LUCIA IMPELLUSO
photographs by **DARIO FUSARO**

Villas and
Gardens
of the Renaissance

Rizzoli
NEW YORK

New York Paris London Milan

Villas and Gardens
of the Renaissance

CONTENTS

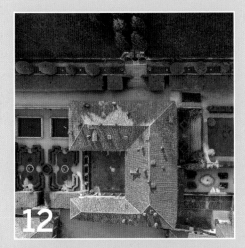

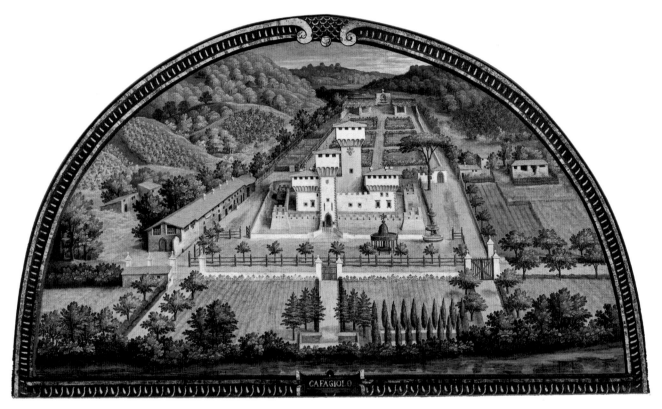

Justus Utens, Villa di Cafaggiolo, circa 1599, the Museo di Firenze com'era, Florence

The concept of the villa goes back to ancient Roman culture and indicates a series of isolated buildings in the countryside, a part of which are used as a residence by the owner (*pars urbana*) and the other part for services and productive activities (*pars rustica*). In time, the structure of these buildings, which at first was rather simple, became more complex and enriched with elegant spaces and ornamentation.

In the second century BC, toward the end

of the Roman Republic, there was a rise in the number of luxurious villas used for rest, *otium*, recreational and intellectual activities, surrounded by the quiet of the landscape, far from the hustle and bustle of the city.

The architecture of the villa changed, and the original shape, which was compact and closed unto itself, was enriched with peristyles, gardens and nymphaeums, porticoes, statues, and rich fountains opening up to the surrounding countryside. The style of the rural building ended up assuming an independent nature, different from the urban one from which it had been conceived, and it would become a fundamental point of reference of Western culture in the later development of the country home.

At the end of the Roman Empire, after the barbarian invasions, the population sought refuge inside fortified castles and hamlets, abandoning the countryside. It was not until the twelfth century, thanks to the rebirth of the city and the consequent flourishing of the communal civilization, that the economy based on the *latifondo* (large estate), at the core of which was the lord's castle, began to disappear. The vast properties were broken up and bought by new citizens who were making their fortunes with industry and commerce. Agriculture underwent a new impetus, and the territory, thanks to tillage, drainage, and renewed cultivations, regained vitality.

Fortified castles and architectures, which were no longer used for defensive purposes, were either abandoned or transformed. In this period the first scientific treatises on farming, vegetable gardens, and flower gardens began to appear. Among them was Pier de' Crescenzi's *Opus ruralium commodorum*, which was highly acclaimed throughout Europe. Praise and rediscovery of the rustic life, on the back of the study of the classics, also involved contemporary literature. In his writings, Petrarch celebrated country life and its benefits. Giovanni Boccaccio set the *Decameron* in a dwelling just outside of Florence, where a group of aristocrats took shelter to escape the plague that had hit the city in 1348. The interest in the villa and in rustic life reached the peak of its expression in the following century, when around the mid-fifteenth century the structures of the castle and the fortified stronghold

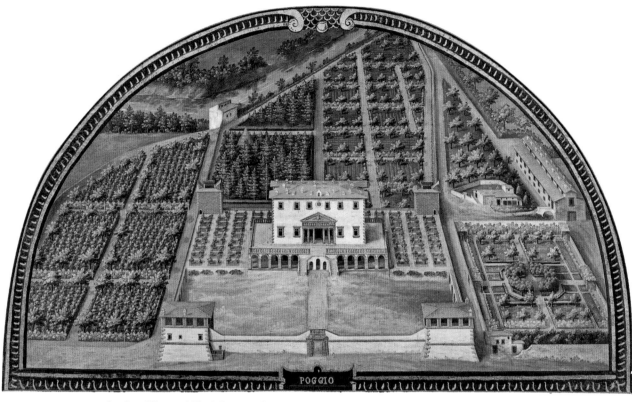

Justus Utens, Villa di Poggio a Caiano, circa 1599, the Museo di Firenze com'era, Florence

embraced the geometric space of the garden and from there the surrounding landscape, renewing that style of architecture and the ancient philosophy of life that accompanied them. The garden became an integrated part of the villa, and as such it abided by certain specific architectural rules. It was based on a regular geometric layout, with low internal walls separating it into sections, thereby creating a cozy space where one could read, meditate, or engage in conversation. Paths had not as yet been conceived to offer a perspectival view of the palazzo, but they had been thought of as a way to connect the various "green rooms," that might even be located at different levels overlooking the exterior.

The landscape itself, properly tended to and arranged over the territory, became a garden, especially in Tuscany, where the conception of the suburban Roman villa in which to retire and devote oneself to *otium*, to escape everyday activities and government duties, came about in Florence at the same time as the rise of the Medici. The oldest of the Medici villas is in Cafaggiolo, in the Mugello Valley, and it still looks like a castle today. It was remodeled by Michelozzo, who chose to emphasize its defensive nature, but also reorganized the farmland, landscaping the garden so that it was a part of the surrounding landscape as well as of the composition overall. The break from the castle tradition took place in the complex of Fiesole, built according to the ideas of Leon Battista Alberti, who had just finished writing *De re aedificatoria*. It was designed based on sloping terraces overlooking the surrounding countryside. The layout and orientation of the garden followed the norms laid down in the Tuscan architect's treatise.

The cultural side of such dwellings was closely linked to the villas that had been frequented from the days

Justus Utens, Villa dell'Olmo a Castello, circa 1599, the Museo di Firenze com'era, Florence

of Cosimo I by philosophers, artists, and intellectuals. The villa in Poggio a Caiano, which was built after 1482 at the behest of Lorenzo the Magnificent and to a plan by Giuliano da Sangallo, was the seat of Neoplatonic teachings. This complex of unusually monumental dimensions was based on elements deriving from classical antiquity, such as the porticoed foundation open on four sides, and the facade featuring an exterior gallery topped by a pediment. The latter, in glazed terracotta, was filled with mythological scenes that alluded to the "choices made by the soul."

The villa also had an enclosure where exotic animals were kept, a gift of the sultan of Babylonia to Lorenzo on the occasion of a visit in 1487. Along with lions and dromedaries, there was also a giraffe immortalized by Andrea del Sarto inside the villa, in one of the frescoes in the halls.

The gardens, as early as the period of the seigneury of Cosimo the Elder, were constantly present in the political plans of the Medici family, especially as a symbol of their power. In particular, it was during the seigneury of Cosimo I that the most famous villas were built, thanks also to the period of economic and social prosperity that had affected Tuscany as well. Spread out over the territory, in the late sixteenth century they formed an economic system and a way to exert political control. Notwithstanding a few basic similarities, the villas and gardens were characterized by a variety of styles, and, most importantly, they expressed specific symbolisms in the way they were laid out, linked to the patrons' needs.

The villa of Castello, which Cosimo I asked Niccolò Tribolo to remodel in 1537, was supposed to fulfill a specific iconography, aimed at celebrating his election as Duke of Florence after victory at the Battle of

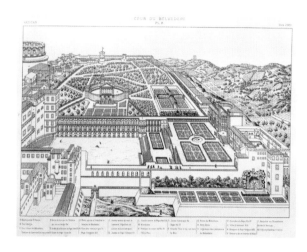

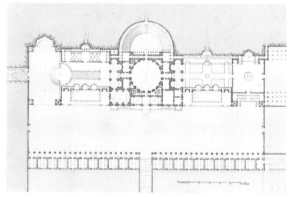

Montemurlo and the resulting resumption of power
by the Medici.

The sculptural decorations represent the most
important places in the duchy, and are arranged so that
they compose the Medici coat of arms. The space of the
villa was organized over three terraces that followed the
sloping nature of the land. The Giardino Grande was
arranged on a central axis decorated with the fountains
of Hercules and Antaeus, a work by Bartolomeo
Ammannati, and with Giambologna's Venere-Fiorenza
fountain, later moved to Petraia.

The *Hercules Slaying Antaeus* sculptural group was
meant to allude to the image of Cosimo defeating
the anti-Medici factions, while Venus-Fiorenza recalled
the image of the city of Florence that in guiding its people
had generated a new spring. The second terrace, located
higher up, was used to cultivate citrus fruits, while
the very last one was set upon a tall support wall
and was named Piano del Gennaio because of the
presence of the eponymous statue made by Bartolomeo
Ammannati. The central path of the large garden ended
below the embankment where the famous Grotto
of the Animals was created, a work begun by Tribolo
and completed by his pupils.

A fundamental stopping-place in the art history
of gardens is the Belvedere, a fully-fledged landscape
project and a model of reference until the Baroque period.

Around 1504, Pope Julius II commissioned Donato
Bramante to conceive a connection between the ancient
core of the papal palace and the villa of Belvedere,
the summer residence that Innocent VIII had had built
and located on a hilltop.

The imposing project that was the result of this was
inspired by the models of Imperial Rome like the Domus
Aurea or the Sanctuary of Fortuna in Palestrina.
By exploiting the natural shape of the site, which sloped
just slightly, Bramante divided the space of the courtyard
into the three levels—closed off by long pathways—of

the corridors of the loggia which allowed for a better and easier connection between the two buildings. The three terraces were connected by flights of stairs, and the space of the lower courtyard, which was used for performances, had seating for the audience. In this new layout Bramante also found a suitable place for Julius II's collection of antiquity, which included, among other things, the famous group of the Laocoön that had been unearthed in a Roman vineyard in 1506. The grandiose dimension of the intervention also reflected the Pope's intentions: the aim of this ambitious project of renewal was to assert the political prestige of the Papal State and the integrity of its territories. Dubbed the first open-air civic theater since antiquity, the first museum, but above all the first realization of the integration between a garden and architecture, the image of the Cortile del Belvedere reflected the further affirmation of human reason, by that time capable of using that reason to control nature itself, reducing it to pure architectural form.

The garden's original layout was altered by the subsequent design by Domenico Fontana involving the construction of a new wing of the library that crossed the Bramantesque courtyard and irremediably spoiled the vision of the whole.

The same celebratory intent underlies the project for Villa Madama, on the slopes of Monte Mario, which Giulio de' Medici, the future Pope Clement VII, commissioned from Raphael about ten years after the project he assigned to Bramante. Directly inspired by the Belvedere, Villa Madama is also inspired by Tuscan tradition and the principles of Leon Battista Alberti. It is a monumental complex set on a rectangular site measuring about 180 meters in width and 40 in depth, positioned transversally with respect to the slope of the hill. It is made up of a central nucleus organized over a series of covered architectures alternating with open-air ones, masterfully combined. The program was inspired by a re-evocation of the ancient villa described

by Pliny the Younger in his letters. All around the main building were a series of gardens and terraces sloping toward the Tiber. When the Urbino artist passed away in 1520, the works continued under the direction of Antonio da Sangallo, but they were interrupted due to the political events that eventually led to the terrible Sack of Rome. The tragic events surrounding the occupation of the Eternal City by Charles V's troops were followed by a profound crisis, which Rome was not able to emerge from until the mid-sixteenth century, discovering when it did that it was more alive than ever. In this new period the villa became a grandiose work of art that involved all the artistic techniques and the literary and scientific knowledge, achieving the absolute highest levels of expression. It is characterized by marvelous and lively decorations and by the use of water in a host of manifestations, creating veritable works of art immersed in greenery, and organized on site plans that were becoming increasingly complex and articulated.

Dated to that period is the complex of Villa d'Este, conceived for Cardinal Ippolito d'Este by Pirro Ligorio, a famous *antiquiario* (antiquarian) and Neapolitan architect, and the author of a massive opus on Roman antiquities.

The majestic garden occupied a vast area that was completely reorganized based on the position of the palazzo, an ancient Benedictine monastery also transformed and renovated by Ligorio. It was organized over a series of spectacular terraces connected by staircases, where the water was expressed in a multitude of fountains, waterfalls, and tubs, surprising water features whose arrangement, along with that of the terraces, hid a complex and varyingly interpreted allegorical meaning. Juxtaposed with the theme of the patron's or the user's choice, who, like Hercules, had to decide whether to undertake the path of vice or that of virtue by following a logical itinerary

Villa d'Este in Tivoli, 17th century, Villa La Pietra, Florence

dictated by the diverse components of the garden, was another esoteric one, accessible to few initiates. It was a sort of journey to the unknown, toward the deepest secrets of nature that led to a knowledge of the mysteries of nature and the psyche via three principal stages, where the four mazes in the garden represented doubt in the endless scientific and cultural research overlapped by the cross of faith, portrayed in the cross-shaped arbor with a dome at the top. The villa dominates from above and inside it the central hall— dining room and reception room—constitutes the central and symbolic space of the building, conceived as the final stop on the path unwinding toward the outside. The frescoes, painted between 1565 and 1568, are a sort of synthesis of the iconography represented in the garden.

A masterpiece of Late Renaissance architecture is the Palazzo Farnese in Caprarola. The palazzo is the result of the conversion of a pre-existing five-sided fortress into a country dwelling, where the modeling of the outer spaces was of essential importance.

This important urban project joined the palazzo and the underlying hamlet into one organic whole, and it is an example of the brilliant work of Vignola, who began designing it in 1566.

The architect lightened up the facade of the building by creating a series of loggias and windows. On the bastions of the fort he created two large square gardens organized into regular compartments with hedges and fruit trees, decorated with fountains and seats on which to rest.

The original unevenness between the fortress and the hamlet was filled by realizing a scenic trapezoidal square with a slight slope, endowed with a series of stairways with two flights leading to the entrance to the building. Hence, the massive block was freed from the isolation that had been determined by its original defense function and connected to the built-up area by a straight road starting from the palazzo.

In Bagnaia, Villa Lante and its garden were arranged over a small slope and the unevenness was solved by creating a series of terraces developed in perspectival succession. Twin architectures much like perspectival backdrops framed the green spaces, which for this same reason were themselves emphasized. Next to the geometric garden is a vast woody area, left in a rustic stage, crossed by paths and dotted with fountains. The garden was conceived as a course that from the world of nature led to that of the art and civilization of humans, crossed and brought to life by a fountain system. Water, after all, is the great protagonist here, the vivifying element: after gushing out from the grotto, through a series of intermediate stops it reaches the fountain of the Mori located at the center of the garden, where it is finally placated.

During the second half of the sixteenth century, the art of the garden was expressed via more elaborate forms, giving rise to the so-called "Mannerist garden." It is very hard to pinpoint the transition from Renaissance language to Mannerist language, which was freer in its expressions. The latter language did not oppose the classical geometric rigor, but, rather, simply renewed the expression, manifesting ever-complicated designs, where the elements involved, i.e. tubs, fountains, and water features, answered to iconographic designs that expressed celebratory or complex allegorical messages. Albeit always seen as a unitary geometric conception, the space expanded and was articulated in clearly defined parts, but ones that did not depend on the garden's overall plan.

The villa addressed by gardens such as these is dictated in the forms of humanistic thinking and by the architectural and literary sources, as well as the ancient treatises. The binomial of the villa and its surroundings spread to the entire country, resulting in extraordinary examples centered on the differences, uniqueness, and history of each individual region, constituting an important point of reference for their subsequent development across Europe.

Georg Braun
and **Frans Hogenberg,**
view of Villa Farnese
and the gardens, from
Civitates Orbis Terrarum,
1572–1617

Raffaellino da Reggio,
view of Villa Lante,
circa 1575, Bagnaia

The earliest records concerning the Mozzoni family date back to the thirteenth century, a period when the Visconti and the Della Torre families were competing for the seigneury of the city of Milan. As soon as the Della Torre rose to power they banished their noble adversaries, who were powerful and whom they feared, from the city. Among those exiled were the Mozzoni, who withdrew to their estates in Varese, where they had been present from the twelfth century.

Villa Cicogna Mozzoni

On the previous spread
View of the western
facade of the palazzo.
Still visible above
the arches is a fresco
enlivened with groups
of putti. Studies by
the experts have
determined that most
of the putti come from
works by Francesco
Primaticcio and
Michelangelo Buonarroti
reproduced in drawings
and engravings
by 16th-century artists

Over the course of the following centuries,

the Mozzoni acquired numerous properties between Arcisate and Bisuschio, which only served to increase their prestige. Exactly when the villa of Bisuschio was built is not known. What we do know is that the brothers Agostino and Antonio Mozzoni owned a hunting lodge there, and that in the fall of 1476, they had the pleasure of hosting the Duke of Milan Galeazzo Maria Sforza for a hunt in the woods nearby. It was on the occasion of that illustrious visit that the family's fate changed favorably. In his diaries, Cicco Simonetta, the duke's powerful *consigliere* and secretary, recorded that while hunting the lord of Milan was attacked by a bear, and that he was saved thanks to the timely reaction of the Mozzoni's mastiff, that bit the ferocious animal. This gave Agostino enough time to quickly react and kill it, although he was still wounded.

To repay the two brothers for their loyalty and bravery, the duke granted them and all their descendants *in infinitum* exemption from all taxes, duties, and property taxes on the places they owned in the Varese area, and on any other territory under Sforza rule. Although the following year Galeazzo Maria Sforza was poisoned to death by his enemies, his heirs confirmed the privileges granted to the family.

The palace as a whole would seem to derive from the subsequent expansions and refurbishments of the hunting lodge that presumably took place around 1535. Dated specifically to August of that same year is an agreement stipulated between the brothers Francesco and Mayno Mozzoni and the brothers Primo and Francesco Biumi, two builders from Varese. According to the contract, the Biumi promised to execute a series of works that had to be finished by June 1536, the penalty being the payment of 25 gold *scudi*. No doubt these and possible other works must have ended by the late 1530s. Indeed, the first record of the villa's existence dates to 1541, the year when the book *Gallorum Insubrum antiquae sedes* was published. This historical-antiquarian book, written by the erudite Milanese clergyman Bonaventura Castiglioni, describes the ancient settlements in the Po Valley. The publication recalls the sumptuous palazzo owned by Mayno Mozzoni as the only monument worthy of note in all of the Ceresio Valley. It can safely be surmised, therefore, that the building was much more structured and elegant than the original hunting lodge.

View of one of the rooms
in the Women's Quarter

View of the western
portico. Dated to
the years around 1580,
the ceiling represents
an arbor brimming
with different types
of fruit, probably
alluding to the richness
and the fertility of the
surrounding lands

VILLA CICOGNA MOZZONI

At the center
of the western portico
is the coat of arms
of the Cicogna Mozzoni,
held up by two cupids
and topped by the crown
of the count

Detail of the eastern
facade of the palazzo,
the so-called Women's
Quarter, which gets
its name from the
frescoes portraying
women looking out from
faux windows toward
the courtyard. Below,
running along the three
facades of the palazzo
facing the courtyard,
is a fragment of the
frieze with cupids

The palace is built on a U plan and has two floors, the result of later works on the original body. The outer facade, which was frescoed at one time, overlooks a small square situated at the end of a perspective tree-lined boulevard, leading from the town directly to the villa. A rusticated portal topped by a shield with the family coat of arms marks the entrance and leads to the central courtyard, or courtyard of honor. From there one can see the layout of the palace, which consists of three blocks of buildings: two to the side with porticoes, and a third in the middle, known as the northern quarter, hence, the typical U shape. A portico was painted on the facade for the purpose of creating symmetry with the other two, as well as to express the stylistic unity of the courtyard and garden complex, which opens up on the fourth side.

All three facades are frescoed: located just above the arches and porticoes is a *fascia* enlivened by groups of boisterous putti holding up nobiliary coats of arms and oval medallions filled with landscapes and mythological deities. The top floor between one window and another is inhabited by gigantic figures whose shapes are still visible today. Some of the windows of the building further up—that

View of the Scalone
d'Onore. The walls
are decorated with
frescoes depicting airy
landscapes, while
the ceiling is decorated
with grotesques
and coats of arms,
and, to the sides, some
of the scenes from
the story of Callisto
in Ovid's
Metamorphoses

View of the large
Salone d'Onore in the
direction of the library.
The walls are adorned
with portraits of the
ancestors, separated
by faux columns with
golden bases and
framed with green
festoons of flowers
and fruit

of the entrance—are painted directly on the facade for a *trompe-l'œil* effect, which is further accentuated by the figures of ladies leaning out and looking downwards or busily carrying out their chores. This wing of the palace is in fact called the Women's Quarter.

The fresco decorations are not the work of one single artist and continue along the way, bringing to life the vaults of the two porticoes and entering the palace as well, embellishing the staircases and the rooms with celebratory and didascalic frescoes, sunlit landscapes, flowers, plants, animal festoons and grotesques. This instills a conversation and a continuing and endless relationship between interior and exterior, between architecture and nature, that bestows the villa-garden complex with truly original coherence and harmonious union. Access to the villa after crossing the courtyard is from the west portico.

The large stairway of honor, whose walls are mostly decorated with lacustrine landscapes, hills, mountains, castles and hamlets framed by faux architecture and stone landings, underscores and enhances the relationship with the surrounding nature, that appears to almost invade the interior of the palazzo, entering through the large windows overlooking the garden at the back.

Northern quarter, room with a fortepiano. The instrument was built in 1798 in Vienna by Anton Walter, one of the most famous Viennese piano makers of his day. He also made the piano acquired by Mozart in 1782, now preserved in the composer's house in Salzburg

View of the library. At the top a frieze frescoed with the Muses and putti. On the fireplace hood is Vulcan in his forge, with Venus and Cupid

The ceiling is frescoed with grotesques and divided into geometric sections featuring the coats of arms of the Mozzoni and other aristocratic families that held an important role in the history of the household. To either side of the ceiling six scenes, three per side, tell the story of Callisto in Ovid's *Metamorphoses*. It is the story of a young nymph who was beloved by Zeus and because of that love was turned into a she-bear by the furious Hera. The union between Zeus and Callisto gave birth to Arcas, who, when he was older, attempted to kill the she-bear not knowing it was his mother. Before that could happen, Zeus quickly turned both of them into a constellation. The representation of the myth in a place visible to all clearly recalls the famous episode of the bear hunt and all the benefits that ensued for the family.

On the top floor to the left is the grand hall of honor, the Salone d'Onore, where the walls are embellished with the portraits of the ancestors separated by faux columns on golden bases and framed in green festoons of flowers and fruit. The grand hall leads into the library dedicated to cultural entertainment and learned dissertations. The interior is dominated by a large fireplace in local stone from Viggiù, while the walls are decorated at the top with a frescoed frieze: amidst images of muses and nobiliary coats of arms, some putti hold up the letters of the alphabet that spell out the words "Venimus ad dulces Parnasi Numina cantus," that is, "we (Muses) have reached the sweet songs of the Parnassus."

The central body of the complex, the so-called northern quarter, is divided into six rooms, which respectively face three to the south and three to the north. The first three are painted with frescoes reproducing elegant damasked drapery in brilliant colors and set in faux architectural ornamentation and columns. Friezes with spirals, plant motifs, grotesques, putti and figures complete the decorations at the top of the walls.

In the walls overlooking the north the drapery disappears but the architectural motifs and friezes, both colored and monochrome, remain.

Lastly, the Women's Quarter unfolds over three rooms arranged in a row and the decorations recall those of the other rooms in the palazzo. Only in the first room is the decoration of the upper *fascia* different from the others: a sunlit landscape runs uniformly along all four walls, on each of which are represented two scenes separated

View of the first room of the Women's Quarter. In the central frieze, to the left is the *Judgement of Paris*, to the right are the *Three Graces*. On the right wall is a glimpse of the *Concordia*, from the *Emblemata* by Andrea Alciato

View of the second room of the northern Quarter, with the double bed, called "of the Cittrona," with an 18th-century canopy

by a tree in the foreground. The majority of the subjects of these representations come from the images of the *Emblemata* written by Andrea Alciato, a famous jurist and scholar who lived in the first half of the sixteenth century. The *Emblemata* is a collection of mottoes and sayings accompanied by images of symbolic and allegorical significance, with short explanatory texts inviting the reader's moral reflection. The volume was highly successful in European Renaissance culture and was translated and published in over one hundred editions. It was also an important source of inspiration for the artists of that day. Based on an analysis of the emblems and the related messages, one might assume the point was to remind and warn the reader to follow virtue.

The Villa Cicogna complex is characterized by strong overall cohesion, in spite of the fact that it was not conceived and planned from one single project. The works that have succeeded one another over time show the owners' immense culture and far-sightedness in following the common lines of intervention that, despite the use of skilled workers and artists with different inclinations and using the variety of artistic languages available at the time, led to the creation of a unitary organism.

Francesco handed the villa down to his daughter Cecilia, who in 1559 married a distant cousin, Ascanio Mozzoni, jurisconsult and figure of note in the Milanese political and cultural scene, whom the sources from that period describe as a cultivated man, a fine humanist, and an excellent poet. The pair are due the creation of the fourth facade overlooking the court of honor, the garden, one of the most interesting and best preserved examples of a Lombard Renaissance garden. The rectangular space is divided in two: the eastern portion hosts two flower-beds bordered by geometric boxwood hedges. A sixteenth-century marble fountain is at the center of each of the flower-beds.

Situated to the west are two rectangular fish ponds bordered by simple stone balustrades brought to life, respectively, by the statues of two putti and a dolphin.

The view of the garden to the east is closed off by tall bay leaf hedges that are interrupted in the areas of the fish ponds, where a spongy tuff wall begins, featuring niches and tondi hosting statues and busts. In the larger niches Hercules fights the Nemean lion at the center, with Diana and Minerva to either side. Around the

The fish pond with statues of two putti holding back a sea monster

View of the wall in spongy tuff with a statue of Hercules fighting the Nemean lion by the sculptor Brunetti from Viggiù

View of the water chain. A double staircase featuring 156 steps, framed between two rows of cypresses, runs along the hill accompanying one of the most famous 16th-century water chains, that falls into the fountain below, decorated with mascarons

base of the wall are eight stone plaques bearing inscriptions, which were probably chosen by Ascanio himself, he and his wife being the sensitive artificers of this site. The tuff facade was made over again between the seventeenth and eighteenth centuries by Francis II, who added the niches where statues and busts still stand today. In any case, much of the garden must have been completed after the deaths of Cecilia (1613) and Ascanio (1593), succeeded by their daughter Angela, who already in 1580, at the age of fifteen, had married the count Giovan Pietro II Cicogna. A noble Milanese family originally from Novara, its members had been high dignitaries of the court and senators; later, being close to the Spanish crown, it was granted important privileges by Charles V.

The new Cicogna Mozzoni branch of the family is celebrated in heraldic coats of arms that are visible in the frescoes at the center of the ceiling of the western portico, amidst flowery arbors, fruit, putti, and animals. It seems the event was also celebrated in two of the eight stone plaques located in the Renaissance garden, where Ascanio's short epigrams suggest the glory of the stork that can never be harmed by violence or civil war, unlike the eagle, which, too sure of

On the previous spread
View of the villa and
the Renaissance garden.
From the late
19th century there were
numerous visitors to
the villa. Mary Logan
Berenson, wife of the
renowned art historian
Bernard, visited
the villa twice in 1904,
and a few years later
purchased the Villa
I Tatti, renovated
by Cecil Pinsent

itself, was defeated in war after celebrating peace. These words likely refer to the tormented discussions about inheritance that involved Cecilia, daughter of Francesco, and her cousin Camilla, daughter of Mayno. An arrogant and astute woman, in order to grab for herself a conspicuous part of the inheritance that was legally not meant to be hers, Camilla had had several shady individuals known to the state of Milan as outlaws threaten Cecilia and Ascanio.

The legal wrangling continued for several years, until Cecilia finally managed to obtain justice.

The Cicogna thus brought the serenity that the Mozzoni had lost, and the plaques were there to remind everyone of this fact in the humanistic manner of that day and age.

If the marriage between Angela and Giovan Pietro changed the name of the complex of Bisuschio, it did nothing to change their and their heirs' love and profuse care of the garden and palazzo. Over the course of the seventeenth century, the garden to the north was landscaped, organized on two tiers so that they were in line with the palace windows. The first, lower level consists of geometric flowerbeds alternating with two small fish ponds. Along the retaining wall of the upper level a gallery had been created, supported by eight pillars covered in limestone sediments and climbing plants, further embellished with water features reproducing a spring and a waterfall. The upper level features geometric flowerbeds dotted at the corners by boxwood spheres.

Angela and Giovan Pietro's son, Francesco, and their grandson Carlo oversaw the landscaping of the garden to the west, which includes a steep hill overlooked by the villa. A double stairway was built here, framing a splendid chain of water in the middle, a motif inspired by that of the Palazzo Farnese in Caprarola. At the top of the staircase a gloriette marks the point of arrival from which there is an excellent view of the villa and of the Ceresio Valley and the surrounding mountains.

Below, a fountain with a mascaron gathers water right before the main room of the villa's piano nobile, where the land was leveled so that its height would be the same as this new portion of the garden. Once again, the relationship between interior and exterior was being renewed, as was the search for the continuity between art and nature that distinguished the complex from its very origins, enchanting visitors over the centuries.

A niche with a fountain arranged along the path connecting the two gardens, at the level of the first floor of the villa

A view of the first level of the northern garden with its typical boxwood spheres

The landscape that developed all around the city of Milan in the fifteenth century was essentially used for farming and consisted of vast estates that stretched into the lowlands and were dotted with small villages. The first villas to be built in this territory in the late fifteenth century were made according to a block structure that derived from the architecture of the castle, characterized by a loggia or portico on the main facade.

Villa Visconti Borromeo Litta

The sculptural group in terracotta, representing the *Rape of the Sabine Women*, decorating the last exedra in the 16th-century garden

View of the facade of the 16th-century building

These buildings were used as hunting

lodges, or for resting, but they were also directly connected with the running of the estates: generally speaking, these were places where one could stay for a short period of time. The Borromeo, merchants and bankers of Tuscan origin, settled in Milan toward the end of the fourteenth century and began increasing their wealth in the early fifteenth century, when Vitaliano I Borromeo was nominated ducal treasurer. Thanks to the favors they received from the Visconti and the resulting feudal privileges, Vitaliano devoted himself to the acquisition of real estate and land on Lake Maggiore, in the area around Milan and close to Lainate. The estate was truly notable, and it was later divided among his numerous children and maintained along with the privileges that had previously been acquired with the advent of the Sforza dynasty as well.

The property in Lainate was inherited by Vitaliano I's grandson, Ludovico, as established by Ludovico the Moor, who intervened as a judge in an inheritance dispute. It was again the Moor, who was trying to offset the growing power of the Borromeo, who determined that Ludovico should acquire the double-barrelled surname Visconti Borromeo, thus initiating a new family descendance. Since the fifteenth century, the farming estates that the Borromeo owned in Lainate must have had the typical manor house, from which the property was managed. Only later would it take on the characteristics of an aristocratic residence.

The Lainate estate, along with other properties, was handed down to Fabio I Visconti Borromeo, councillor to the Spanish king. Fabio I inherited it in 1569, but he died that same year, so the estate ended up in the hands of his son Pirro I. The villa was first described in a document from 1569, which carefully detailed the property inherited by Fabio I. Thanks to this description, scholars have managed to find proof, later confirmed with restoration, that an original villa was located there, one of those landlord's houses for utilitarian purposes that were rather common in the Lombard countryside. Pirro I thus began improving the conditions of the rural estates, succeeding in increasing their income, some of which came from the advantageous marriages he had underwritten. In 1584, upon the death of his wife Ippolita Porro, he became the sole administrator of the substantial patrimony for his daughter Costanza. He later married Camilla Marino, a member of one of Milan's richest families, which

only served to further consolidate his financial status. In the meantime, Pirro I achieved notable results professionally as well: he was nominated Knight of Santiago, he became a member of the Council of the Sixty Decurions, one of the city's most powerful administrative organs, and he also became a councillor to the Gonzaga of the city of Mantua, which was a part of the State of Milan. This social ascent was compelling, and it paved the way to the highest echelons of Milanese aristocracy. Thanks to the position he achieved, Pirro began to acquire property and land and to put his properties in order, so that they complied with the social level and economic power he had achieved, as tradition dictated. Thus, between 1585 and 1596, he devoted himself to restoring the complex of Lainate, and purchased the famous Villa Pliniana on Lake Como, along with a few other buildings in Milan. In Lainate Pirro started rebuilding the manor house that was already there, and dealing with the gardens. The ancient residence was completely transformed by the architect Martino Bassi, who was especially famous in Milanese and Lombard circles for his church architecture. Bassi had already worked for the Visconti when he remodeled the family's summer house near Monza, according to a project that was very similar to the one in Lainate.

The sixteenth-century building, which was originally meant to be

The southern facade
of the nymphaeum.
It was originally built
with facing bricks,
probably as part
of a recovery of the
ancient Roman thermal
baths. Toward the late
18th century, the facade
was reconstructed
to create a "place
of water" via the use
of travertine, shells,
and reliefs depicting
the water deities

a *riposteria* (storage area), features a rectangular plan and has two floors, with a portico supported by coupled columns in granite. It is likely that this part already existed in the fifteenth century, as proven by the traces of painted geometric motifs on the wooden beams of the coffered ceiling that were discovered under the frescoes. On the other side of the portico is a circular atrium that, to the left, overlooks a single room and, to the right, several rooms. The ceilings are all frescoed with hunting scenes, as well as with figures and tales from mythology. The frescoes have been attributed to Pier Francesco Mazzucchelli, called Morazzone, and to two other less famous painters, Agostino Lodola and Giovanni Battista Maestri, called il Volpino. The portico leads to the staircase to the upper floor, where the ceiling with lunettes is frescoed by sixteenth-century decorations.

The Villa Visconti Borromeo, after the first works organized by Pirro I, underwent numerous other renovations and additions over the following centuries. The architectural complex was expanded via the construction of the so-called "Quarto nuovo" (New Quarter), an eighteenth-century palazzo closing off the entrance courtyard. Its being handed down to the Litta family brought about further improvements and the expansion of the gardens. The original sixteenth-century site was set on a single perspective north-south axis

containing the palazzo, the nymphaeum, and the exedra at the end, decorated with tuff and mineral aggregations hosting the terracotta sculptural group of the *Rape of the Sabine Women* made by the circle of Giambologna.

The sixteenth-century garden, in addition to the nymphaeum, was divided into four formal flower-beds and decorated at the center with over one hundred lemon and citrus plants cultivated in vases. It seems that Pirro was particularly devoted to the garden, as can be inferred from his correspondence with the Duke of Mantua Vincenzo I Gonzaga, a plant expert and patron of famous botanists.

Within the garden as a whole, the nymphaeum is of essential importance, in that it serves as the visual, spatial and architectural fulcrum of the entire system. It also expresses its twofold function: the recreational and playful function of its water, and the scientific and cultural one that was typical of the Renaissance, that is, collecting art objects and rarities. The building, which was designed by Martino Bassi and finished in 1587, features a rectangular plan with a series of spaces, rooms, and grottos covering a surface area of almost 1000 square meters. At the center is a room with an octagonal plan, called the Sala dei Quattro Venti, closed off by a dome and painted with illusionistic effects, and ending with a lantern. On

On the previous spread
One of the rooms
decorated in mosaic

the walls are several niches that at one time hosted bronze statues representing the winds blowing unexpected spurts of water onto unwitting visitors. Gushes of water also came from the center of the floor and the entrance to the room. The central room was the start of a path all along the internal rooms whose floors, walls, and ceilings are decorated with white quartz and black limestone pebbles so that they create arabesque, floral, and zoomorphic motifs.

The ceiling of the south-facing rooms are the work of Camillo Procaccini, a Bolognese painter who was trained in the artistic circles of the Emilian city, and was summoned to Milan by Pirro I himself. After Lainate he started an important career in Milan along with his brothers Giulio Cesare and Carlo Antonio, mostly working for a religious commission having to do with the strictures of the Counter-Reformation.

The Bolognese painter masterfully used the tempera technique to design, in the tenuous colors of turquoise, sienna, and ochre, the white pebbles arranged beforehand to portray images from classical mythology and medieval bestiaries. The environments thus decorated were destined to host Pirro I's collection, which included works by such artists as Bronzino, Correggio and Bernardino Luini, alternating with rooms that held natural curiosities and automatons. All the objects were lost from the mid-nineteenth century onwards following the family's economic decline. These rooms of artistic and scientific interest alternated with those with water features, where water was the dominant element represented by spurts, gushes, and showers. The intent was playful, aimed at arousing the wonder and the bewilderment of the viewer, according to the rules of the Mannerist garden.

In the Stanza del Temporale a rain and thunder effect were created. In the Cortile delle Piogge, an open-air octagonal room, the water was generated by adjusting the intensity of the rain and the rainbows thanks to a sophisticated hydraulic system that has since been lost. Lastly, there are the grottos, a hemicycle from which a labyrinthine system of galleries spreads out, covered with coffered ceilings decorated with stalactites, calcareous rocks, travertine, shell and colored stone compositions, brought to life by naiads and satyrs. The movement of the waters between fountains and games must have been quite notable, even before the work that was done in the eighteenth century. The hydraulic waterworks were based on

Hydraulic automata
in the room known
as the "grottino"

Mosaic of the Gallery

On the following spread
View of the garden. At the rear the northern front of the nymphaeum and to the right the 18th-century fountain of Galatea

the extraction of the water from a well, thanks to a complex pump system that was set in motion by animal power. The water aspired by the well reached a tub at the top of an approximately twenty-meter-tall tower called the Torre dell'Acqua. When the water then fell by way of a complex distribution network, it made it possible to achieve the pressure required to set the games and fountains in motion. It seems that Pirro accompanied his guests along a carefully determined path that only he knew about. The gradual discovery while crossing the series of rooms, the sought-after surprise effect, the decorations of the grottos, all this evoked and harkened back to the garden of the Pratolino, but also to Boboli and Castello, that Pirro must have had the chance to see personally thanks to the good relationship between his family and the Medici.

The visitor must have experienced wonder and astonishment before each of these gimmicks, observing a miniature world that allowed them to discover the harmony of nature in the formation of rocks with the elements that make them up and in the multiform appearances of water.

Not to mention the splendid collection of paintings, rare objects, and hydraulic devices, a late-Renaissance Wunderkammer and an open book on the world. An artificial world where Pirro I managed to dominate nature and its elements, by celebrating himself as being a cultivated and rich member of the Milanese and Lombard aristocracy. Such a cabinet of curiosities would remain until the late nineteenth century, and be enriched over the course of the century with extravagant and precious objects, ethnic and naturalistic curiosities that would only serve to further revive the original relationship between nature and artifice that characterized the collection from the time it was born in the sixteenth century.

The nymphaeum of Villa Litta, after a period of neglect that affected the complex as a whole, underwent major restoration work starting from the early 1980s. Once the structure and ceilings were consolidated, work began to restore the mosaics of the interiors and the water features, which were opened to the public once more in 1996. Since then, the nymphaeum has been open to tourists and curiosity-seekers, arousing in them that sense of wonder and surprise that had made it so famous when it was first created in the late Renaissance.

The water features were one of the main attractions of the villa until the late 19th century

Water features in the eastern galleries

While Rome was the symbol of antiquity in the fifteenth century, where the ancient manifested itself, Padua was the place where that same antiquity was studied in history, archaeology, and philosophy. The Studium, the University of Padua, one of the oldest universities in Europe, proved to be an important point of reference for humanistic culture.

LUVIGLIANO

Villa dei Vescovi

On the previous spread
View of the complex
of Villa dei Vescovi.
To the left are
the stairs that led
to the original entrance,
on the southern side
of the villa

The attempt to reconstruct the past

beyond the literary dimension in order to turn to the visual sources that were available, such as architecture, epigraphs, coins, and art objects, could vaunt a tradition that dated all the way back to the late thirteenth century. This antiquarian identity was renewed over time until it was wholly expressed in the sixteenth century when, after the War of the League of Cambrai and the subsequent regaining of its dominion over the terra firma, Venice initiated a political and military overhaul of the territories of the State. During this period, Padua witnessed considerable growth in its constructions and in its economy. Nobles and illustrious patrons contributed to reshaping its look. Pietro Bembo, the famous cardinal, grammarian, and writer, who had received his education in Padua, in 1532 chose to move to the city, bringing with him his remarkable art and book collection. An important figure of reference for classicist culture, Bembo was highly esteemed and was considered an authority in the city's intellectual circles. Among the intellectuals and patrons who were active in Padua at the time, Alvise Cornaro was particularly distinguished. Cornaro was a gentleman scholar of Venetian origins, and a staunch supporter of investments in agriculture and in the reclamation of the marshlands, from which a new profit could be made. He was also one of the first to devote himself to similar operations on his own property, near Codevigo, which went from being unproductive marshland to a thriving agricultural center.

A unique, multifarious figure, Cornaro was practical, concrete, and visionary, a protector and friend of artists and literati, and the author of theoretical writings on agriculture, architecture, and a sober life. In 1529, he was nominated administrator of the estate of the curia by the powerful Padua cardinal Francesco Pisani. Also part of the plan to reorganize the vast landed properties of the Padua bishopric was the construction of the summer residence of the bishops in Luvigliano di Torreglia, on the Euganean hills. Luvigliano was especially cherished by the humanists, for they believed, albeit erroneously, that it was the site of the Livianum, the country abode of the famous Latin historian Titus Livius, a native of Padua.

The new villa was built between 1535 and 1543, and for its design Cornaro turned to Giovanni Maria Falconetto, a painter and architect that the nobleman had already hired for other commissions. Giovanni Maria Falconetto was born in 1468 in Verona, where he was trained

Entrance from
the western loggia

Western loggia
with frescoes by
Lambert Sustris

VILLA DEI VESCOVI

View of the Chamber
of the Bishop

On the previous spread
Sala delle Figure
with frescoes
by Lambert Sustris

as a painter and antiquarian. In 1517, forced to abandon his city for political reasons, he headed to Rome, where he had the opportunity to familiarize with and study antiquity as interpreted by the new language of Bramante. Upon returning to Padua he began working for Alvise Cornaro, a patron and friend, whom he remained close to until his death.

The contract for the villa in Luvigliano was signed in February 1535, after Falconetto's death in early January of the same year.

The agreement was therefore confirmed on the basis of a project that already existed and that did not exclude Falconetto's contribution. Scholars agree on attributing the project to the architect, for his language can be recognized in numerous elements of the design. For instance, he had a very particular way of dealing with the architectural details in the capitals and bases, directly inspired by the Roman monuments of Verona that Falconetto, of Veronese origin, was accustomed to drawing and then using as models.

The Cornaro and Falconetto villa does not correspond to what we can see today, which is the result of subsequent works. It was simpler, and consisted of a cubic volume set on a base with a square plan with a larger side.

The villa's piano nobile was lightened up on the eastern and western facades by loggias overlooking the landscape. The complex was built over a fifteenth-century construction: a block with a square base and a space at the center that was also square and open, which Falconetto harkened back to in the structure, expanding and encircling it on all four sides by a continuous portico with vaults. The open space of the basement corresponded to a specular one on the piano nobile, almost certainly a hanging courtyard that cast light on the floor itself and on the one underneath it, thanks to purposefully designed openings, some of which can still be seen today. The entrance to the villa was from the southern side, and it was marked by the presence of two stone benches, an erudite nod to the seating of the Roman *domus*, where the *clientes* waited to be received by the owners of the house. The connection to the piano nobile was presumably via internal staircases.

The works should have been almost completed in the summer of 1542, when Francesco Pisani removed Cornaro from the job of supervising the project, and turned to Giulio Romano instead, asking him for a consultancy regarding the villa. The records in fact show

that Giulio Romano inspected Luvigliano, where the architect of the Gonzaga made some changes to the interiors. Based on an analysis of the most recent restorations it would seem that the arches on the southern facade were originally open, and that they were closed only later with the insertion of windows. Furthermore, of the five arches making up the facade, the two to the sides of the one in the middle are blind, seeing that the side walls of the central room were erected right behind them. This led to the idea that a variation was made to the internal distribution of the building originally conceived by Falconetto. A variation that can be attributed to Giulio Romano, who also dealt with the external base, reinforcing the walls with rustication.

The process to complete the villa took place in the 1560s, when the architect Andrea da Valle changed the orientation of the building and created a new entrance to the west: a vast courtyard through which to enter, surrounded by crenelated walls, interrupted by three portals in the Ionic order, leading to the monumental stairway into the building.

The interiors, modified in the seventeenth century by the impluvium at the center of the main corridor, were painted by Lambert Sustris, a famous Flemish painter who was very active in the 1540s in Padua, and had already worked on the decorations inside Alvise Cornaro's odeon, and in the Sala dei Giganti in the Palazzo del Capitanio.

The frescoes of Villa dei Vescovi, most of which were finished

in 1543, have been tampered with over time, owing also to the variations in the internal distribution of the rooms. The Sala di Apollo e Orfeo, for instance, appears to be adorned according to two different types of decorations, evidently conceived for two different rooms that were once separate. The room containing figures *all'antica* is the best preserved. This was supposed to be a place in which to greet guests, as suggested by the frescoes themselves, inspired by Roman tradition. The walls are frescoed and have faux white marble pilasters framing faux niches with statues, and aediculae containing elegantly dressed male and female figures, portrayed posing solemnly against a background of faux drapery. The figures are those of illustrious people, kings, queens, emperors and empresses, whose manner is reminiscent of the Sala dei Giganti in the ancient Palazzo del Capitanio in Padua, where Sustris himself had worked. Above the ledge is a long frieze consisting of squares brimming with congeries of antiquarian objects, which take turns with airy landscapes inhabited by ruins and figures; in some of them we can recognize deities and their stories in mythology. In the adjacent, smaller room, referred to as the Sala del Putto due to the presence of a small putto leaning up against a column and seated on the parapet, the landscapist illusion is expanded until it occupies the entire wall, where faux arcades open up.

Especially evocative is the sweeping garden at the entrance, divided into four large sections by perpendicular paths that lead to the open doors in the walls: one of them is directed toward the garden and is aligned with the villa; another one connects the villa to the *barchesse*, while the third one is a belvedere overlooking the vineyards below.

Lambert Sustris,
landscape scenes
in the frieze
in the Sala delle Figure

The garden consists of simple areas filled with grass along with a few nineteenth-century conifers and lemons in vases, reminiscent of the ancient sixteenth-century garden. What makes the villa in Luvigliano a truly special place is the site where it rises up and its relationship with the surrounding landscape. It is a villa that was built for the purpose of viewing, admiring, and immersing oneself in nature.

A site in the manner of what Petrarch had described, where the spirit, regaining its strength, could find new vigor and inspiration. Cornaro and Trissino, moreover, were among the first to transfer the language of classical architecture to the Veneto countryside, thereby creating an important precedent for all the abodes that would soon be scattered throughout the territory in the region, and whose architect, Andrea Palladio, had received his training in their school. The famous Vicenza-born architect developed this theme by going further and stressing the villa's productive side. Indeed, he made the *barchesse* and the manor house into a single organism: not just a villa where you could rest, but also a villa in which to work and manage the lands. However, it was the Complesso dei Vescovi that Palladio had in mind when he designed the famous Rotonda, which faces Luvigliano, not just for the architecture's compact structure and dominant position, but also for the renewed relationship with the surrounding environment.

Antechamber
of the Chamber
of the Bishop

Entrance to the villa

**On the following
spread**
Villa dei Vescovi viewed
from the western facade

In the year 1200, the powerful Della Torre family owned the seigneury of Milan, which they had taken control of after defeating the Visconti and banishing from the city any families that supported them. The fate of the two families swung in favor of one or the other until toward the mid-fourteenth century, when the Visconti definitively gained authority over the capital of Lombardy, and cast the Della Torre from the city. The family then moved east, toward Friuli, to Verona and Gorizia.

FUMANE

Villa della Torre

Giulio della Torre was a descendant of the

Veronese line of the family. He was a jurisconsult, a scholar, and a fine humanist, and in 1504 in a sumptuous ceremony he married Anna Maffei, the only child of Guido Antonio Maffei, the descendant of an ancient patrician family from Verona, and the owner of a manor house, and the land that came with it near Fumane, in Valpolicella. The old residence was reconverted into a villa after 1530 by Giulio and his sons Girolamo and Francesco, who during that period both held important positions with the Verona curia that gravitated around Bishop Gian Matteo Giberti. A lover of humanistic culture, Giberti had been the promoter of an important program for religious, cultural and social renewal in his diocese. Those were the years just before the Council of Trent, marked by a profound religious crisis and by the upheaval caused by the Protestant Reform, which Giberti had tried to quell with a series of reforming measures.

The project for the Villa della Torre complex was inspired by the writings of Vitruvius on the houses of the ancients, filtered by the Renaissance spirit vis-à-vis a return to the vestiges of classical antiquity.

The layout develops over a series of open spaces arranged in a row: five descending levels that follow the slight slope of the land and are connected by relatively small stairways. The fifth level, visible in an ancient eighteenth-century map and indicated as *brolo*, corresponded to the vast area now cultivated with vineyards, located opposite the main entrance and separated from it by a path.

The abode is the heart and soul of the complex and it consists of two compact, symmetrical buildings that unfold around a central porticoed peristyle, after the model of ancient Roman homes. The fourteenth-fifteenth-century manor house was englobed in the block to the east. Buildings and open spaces were visually connected by a central perspectival axis that joined them in a single organism.

Not too far away is a temple featuring an octagonal plan attributed by Alessandro Vasari to Michele Sanmicheli, a famous Verona architect who, along with Jacopo Sansovino, contributed to disseminating the motifs of Roman antiquity in Northern Italy, expressing them according to Renaissance language. The building is preceded by a tripartite loggia with a Venetian window in the

One of the monstrous fireplaces with a Satanic face decorating the rooms in the villa

View of the peristyle

middle and two rectangular spaces to either side, topped by niches that were originally filled with statues.

The general feature of the complex is the use of rustic ashlar, which is present in the stone pillars supporting the arcade of the central courtyard in the temple facade and in the ornamentation. Beyond the peristyle, toward the garden there is a further architectural structure made up of a fish pond crossed by a small bridge with three arches. The uniqueness of the area, the image of the internal courtyard opening onto the garden by way of the fish pond, and the deliberate use of rustic ashlar evoke the language of Giulio Romano and in particular his work on the Palazzo Te in Mantua. The various studies on the matter generally affirm that the layout at Fumane was suggested by Giulio della Torre himself, a man of erudition, a scholar of antiquity, an inventor of medals and a member of the cultural milieu that revolved around Gian Matteo Giberti, for whom Francesco della Torre, Giulio's son, was personal secretary for almost eighteen years. Leaving aside the question of its attribution, the villa is a truly unique and original episode in the scenario of Venetian villas in that period. Akin to the layout of the residence, the gardens as well are characterized by a truly particular organization. The structure, which develops over five rectangular terraces, is the result of a unitary project. Having gone past the ancient *brolo*, a hemicycle staircase leads from the main entrance to the first garden, overlooking the facade of the villa, made up of two lawns separated by the entrance path and surrounded by a low fence decorated with stone spheres. After crossing the portal topped by a tympanum, the visitor enters the central peristyle, where the space is marked by rusticated pilasters that are arranged at regular intervals along the perimeter of the portico. All that is left of the original decor are some stone vases and a column fountain in the middle. The portico was once embellished with a series of ancient busts, part of the family's antiquarian collection that it appears was meant to be housed in the villa.

In addition to the peristyle, beyond another portal that is symmetrical to the former one, is the level that features the fish pond, its parapets are once again decorated by a stone sphere motif.

A double flight of stairs at the center, or one of the two arranged to the sides, lead to the floor below. This last part of the garden was decorated with a fountain in the middle, situated so as to conclude

a waterway that, starting from above, crossed the peristyle and was collected in the fish ponds. From there it flowed down into the grotto below through two cracks in the shape of small cascades, before reaching the central fountain, from which it then flowed out to irrigate the fields. The grotto, located between the two central staircases that branch out from the level of the fish pond, is still visible today, and deemed one of the oldest among those in existence in the Veneto. The entrance is distinguished by a rough mass of rocks resembling an anthropomorphic mascaron, a sort of monster with its mouth agape that seems to have been turned to stone by some mysterious spell.

The interior develops over an irregular octagonal plan with a pillar at the center holding up the vault. The walls must have been decorated with pumice and spongy stone materials, snails, quartzes, and river pebbles, which modulated the gleam of the sources of light creating exciting luminous effects. The finishings were an imitation of the nymph caves described by the ancients and revived in the contemporary architecture treatises.

On the wall opposite the entrance is another sneering mascaron with its jaws open around two small balustrades, from which the water from the fish pond would flow out and supply the central fountain that no longer exists.

Such fearful figures in the grotto can also be seen inside the villa in the effigies of the four fireplaces, characterized by mascarons with their jaws wide open located on the ground floor and overlooking the peristyle. These are unusual images, poised between plants and animals, between the human figure and the anthropomorphic one, which in their oversized dimensions upset the harmony of the surrounding space. Everything seems to harken back to the theme of Ovidian metamorphosis and transformation, which can also be seen in the frescoes of the palazzo walls in Mantua, the idea for which inspired the villa.

Hence, this piece of architecture in Fumane aims to reaffirm an interpretation of the ancient villa according to the canons dictated by Vitruvius, at the same time offering a further message linked to the grotesque and visionary figures in the grotto and on the fireplaces: as if the classicism the villa is steeped in sought to go further, at the same time manifesting the idea of something unsettling and threatening that appeared to loom over these spaces in classical style.

Bridge over
the fish pond

If we are to understand the allegorical message that seems to hide behind that of derision and irony, we cannot ignore the historical and cultural environment in which the artists worked. As we said before, Giulio della Torre was a man of culture, a writer, an antiquarian collector, while his sons, Francesco and Girolamo, gravitated around the figure of Bishop Giberti, with whom the brothers collaborated closely. Those were the years prior to the Council of Trent, years when the Christian religion was being deeply torn from within, undergoing upheaval that the Della Torre experienced personally as members of the cultural circle of Giberti, where the study and in-depth knowledge of the holy scriptures were encouraged.

The motif of the monster of Fumane, seen from the Christian point of view of weakness on Earth and the quest for salvation, harkens back to the image of the infernal monster of Nordic inspiration that swallows the damned it holds in its jaws, an image that was reproduced in numerous paintings and sculptures from both the Middle Ages and the Renaissance. Hence, in Fumane the path is a rising one, which starts from the lower garden, the image of an Eden-like, happy place, that is deceiving, however, because it is threatened by the presence of the infernal Monster looming over it. It is a sort of

Interior of the "infernal"
grotto with the
mascaron of a monster

Fireplace with a roaring
face symbolizing evil

Rear facade of the villa
with a bridge over
the fish ponds leading
to the peristyle

enchanted garden, where temptation and sin can be found. From the infernal grotto the path leads to the upper level, to the spaces in the peristyle featuring four monsters guarding over the fire. Two of them represent a diabolic face and a roaring lion, both of which symbolize evil, while the other two represent a unicorn, a famous Christological symbol and, hence, the image of good. It has thus been inferred that the four fireplaces allude to the eternal struggle between good and evil. Once the magic and spells of the spirits of hell have been overcome, the destination can only be a spiritual one: the Sanmichelian temple rising up in the highest and farthest part of the Grotta dell'Orco. Underscoring the antithetical relationship between the grotto and the temple is their common octagonal layout: with irregular, undefined contours, the image of satanic imperfection, the grotto is offset by the geometric perfection of the temple, the image of celestial perfection.

A path of moral elevation, that contrasts the image of futile wandering and bewilderment suggested by the circular movement around the pillar supporting the cave as opposed to straight, direct movement leading to salvation. A vision that, on the one hand, embraces the law that says one must build according to Vitruvian classicism, and, on the other, abides by the theoretical theme of moral teaching, which was in no way removed from the climate of moral renewal promoted in Verona by Gian Matteo Giberti almost a decade before the Council of Trent established new rules for living the Christian life.

The date of the villa is still uncertain, even though the documents show that in the 1540s work was already in progress. It was unquestionably finished in 1559, the year when Onofrio Panvinio painstakingly described the villa of Fumane in his work *Antiquitatum Veronensium Libri VIII*. What we do know is that the villa of Fumane represents an isolated episode in the history of the architecture of Venetian villas. It is worthwhile noting, however, that a few years later Andrea Palladio conceived Villa Sarego, which was never finished. Villa Sarego takes its distance from the conventional Palladian language: it is organized around a large quadrangular peristyle, whose style and materials curiously share something with Fumane in the reference to the ancient abode and the copious use of rustic ashlar.

Among the villas built according to the designs of Palladio in the Venetian hinterland, Villa Barbaro in Maser is one of the most famous. Elegantly set on a slight slope of the Trevigiano hills, it also owes its renown to the wonderful frescoes by Paolo Veronese decorating the interiors. Designed in the sixteenth century, the complex is the result of the collaboration between the architect and his patrons, Daniele and Marcantonio Barbaro.

MASER

Villa Barbaro

On the previous spread
View of the facade
of the villa

The corner capital,
a nod to the Temple
of the Virile Fortune
in Rome, is a solution
that Palladio used in
other projects as well

Detail of the facade
of the central body
of the villa. In the
foreground the statue
of Juno that, together
with that of Jupiter,
welcomes visitors
at the entrance

Members of one of the oldest Venetian

families, the two erudite noblemen were devoted to humanistic studies and ancient architecture. Daniele had been educated at the University of Padua, where he had studied philosophy, astronomy, and mathematics. Between 1548 and 1550, he had been the Venetian ambassador to the English court.

Upon returning to his homeland, although he had access to a number of prestigious posts, he preferred to accept the position of Patriarch of Aquileia. This would allow him to devote himself to humanistic studies and to his many cultural interests and activities which entailed, among other things, the translation of Vitruvius' *De architectura*, published in 1556. The drawings in the plates contained in the volume that reconstruct ancient buildings were mostly made by Andrea Palladio, who had been collaborating with Daniele Barbaro since 1550. Marcantonio Barbaro, Daniele's younger brother, as well as being an illustrious politician, had been the promoter of some important public works in the Serenissima Republic, such as the Church of the Redeemer and Rialto Bridge. Educated according to humanistic principles like his brother, he nourished a deep passion for architecture and sculpture, which he practiced at an amateur level.

The design of the villa was influenced by the two brothers' many interests. Scholars have in fact discovered it to contain some unconventional solutions and discrepancies with respect to Palladio's other inventions. And we should not overlook the fact that Andrea found himself working in the presence of a pre-existing manor house that had belonged to Francesco Barbaro, the father of the two patrons who inherited it when he died in 1549. Shortly afterwards, the Barbaro brothers devoted themselves to landscaping the rural estates, and Daniele, who seems to have assumed a more important role in that experience, was given the opportunity to translate into practice what he was studying about Vitruvius and classical architecture. Assigning the task to Palladio, who was already collaborating with him, proved to be the most logical and consequential choice.

In 1554, just before he devoted himself to designing the villa, Palladio was in Rome with his erudite patron to complete the translation and revising of Vitruvius' treatise, which would be published in a few years' time. There he had the chance to visit the construction sites of Villa Giulia and to talk to Pirro Ligorio, who was working on a project to complete the gardens of Villa d'Este in Tivoli: a grandiose hydraulic

creation based on major removal of the land, a sort of miracle that left Daniele Barbaro speechless as well. The realization of a semicircular nymphaeum at the back of Villa Maser can only have been the result of that trip to Rome. Dug into the side of the hill at the level of the piano nobile, it overlooked a hemicyclic vat from which, thanks to a complex hydraulic system, the water flowed into the villa and was used for domestic purposes. From the residence it then reached the front garden, where it supplied the eight fountains there, and from those fountains it flowed into the fountain of Neptune, on the other side of the public street, symbolizing the sea where all the water is collected, after which it reached the fields.

The conception of the nymphaeum, an unusual element in Palladio's production, is believed to be due to Daniele Barbaro. Instead, the statues that adorn it, which are generally attributed to the sculptor Alessandro Vittoria, seem to be the work of Marcantonio Barbaro, who enjoyed dabbling in the art of sculpture. The statues are arranged in several niches made on the front of the nymphaeum and represent the Olympian gods. An epigram at the bottom of each of the figures reveals their identity. At the center of the hemicycle an arch watched over by two telamons leads inside a grotto whose vault once featured several frescoes depicting nymphs, almost certainly painted by Paolo Veronese. These were repainted several times and finally plastered over during the course of the restoration work carried out in the 1930s. The nymphaeum is connected to the central body of the house, which for this reason appears to be unusually deep. The Vicenza architect maintained the perimeter of the old manor house and added a further building, divided into three rooms overlooking the small garden. By choosing this solution, Palladio also succeeded in connecting to the main building the two *barchesse* located to the sides that had originally been isolated. Revealing his great skill at adapting to the various characteristics of the site, he managed to create an original example of a villa-farmhouse, where the manor house and the side porticoes formed a harmoniously compact architectural unit. The side wings ended with two *colombaie* (top floors), crowned by a tympanum below which was a sundial embellished with astrological symbols.

The facade of the central building, which is taller and in a more prominent position, is divided into four Ionic engaged columns holding up a triangular pediment brimming with decorations. Moreover, the archivolt of the window at the center of the piano nobile interrupts

View of the Sala
a Crociera with frescoes
by Veronese. Originally,
frescoes were present
also on the vaults
in this room

the continuous line of the pediment, an "error" that Palladio would correct in the plate illustrating the villa in his treatise, where the facade appears to be regular and proportioned, more in keeping with the thinking of the great artist, who would have never committed an "illegal" *faux pas* contradicting the rules of classical architecture.

Evidently, the patron's idea differed from what Palladio had in mind. The architect staunchly believed that architecture was superior to all the other arts. For Daniele Barbaro, instead, the complex was meant to represent the union of all the arts by way of the massive use of decoration, sculpture, and painting. The window was then modified so as to give more light to the frescoes inside.

In spite of this, what still emerges in the villa is Palladio's language, a new language that, although it did not repudiate the Roman and Tuscan models, was born and developed in a cultural context that differed from that of Central Italy. The Veneto of the fourteenth and sixteenth centuries did not have gardens that were similar in terms of structure to those of the Roman princes, with terraces and water features. The noble landowners had other interests. Their lands had been drained with great effort, all the water had been re-

A gentleman returning
from the hunt

A view of the Stanza
del Tribunale dell'Amore

moved, they had been reclaimed and endowed with a canal system
that could make them fertile. They were not interested in creating
vast parks, that would have meant spending lots of money and re-
quiring a workforce that could otherwise be used to till the fields. Nor
were they interested in building representative dwellings, exclusively
dedicated to otium, rest, and holidays. The house was also meant to
be a place where one could administer one's estate, a sort of general headquarters from which to coordinate and oversee the family's
agricultural production. The aristocratic families that moved from
Venice to the terra firma needed buildings in which family, servants,
and livestock could all live together; practical, functional buildings,
but ones that at the same time could reflect the culture and the mag-
nificence of the owners by harkening back to the legacy of classical
antiquity. Palladio, who was born and grew up in such an environment, became the spokesperson for those needs. The new villa had
to have a pre-eminent and central position within the farming estate,
and it had to unite both the rustic buildings and the manor house in
a single complex.

The buildings had to be located in the surrounding landscape
without being overbearing; rather, they had to seek a rapport of re-
ciprocal harmony. In planning the building, the artist had to examine
the characteristics of the place and create a great number of compositions, adapting them to the needs of the surroundings. In villas
of this kind the architectural motifs inspired by antiquity, such as
pediments, columns, and tympana, were cleverly integrated with the
parts of the estate that were used for farming and served as facili-
ties, a reflection of the Vitruvian principles of utility and simplicity.
It goes without saying that the gardens of villas such as these were
not founded on complex technical devices or conceived to manifest
political authority. The garden was not meant to complete the architecture; rather, it was meant to be a part of the natural landscape,
connecting the architectural framework to the cultivated land, to the
hills, and to the woods. In Palladio's villas, the relationship with nature was very strong and the garden was meant to reveal the extent
of the property, to suggest its economic prosperity. From his abode
the lord could admire a view of cultivated nature and his estate in
general: nature was never forced, and the buildings well adapted to
the features of the land itself. Although gardens are rarely mentioned
in the *Four Books on Architecture*, the reader does perceive a few of

On the previous spread
Vault of the Stanza del
Tribunale dell'Amore.
A young bride kneeling
between her husband
and the defender is
about to be judged.
To the sides of the
main scene, the ceiling
features vineyards
that visually stretch
all the way to the sky

Giustina Giustiniani,
wife of Barbaro,
with the nurse,
detail of the ceiling
of the Sala dell'Olimpo

their unique features, such as their size, which is generally modest, and their enclosure, not too high up, so as to avoid closing them off, actually establishing a dialectical relationship between the agricultural environment and the architecture. This element is well expressed in Villa Barbaro Maser, one of the few to which Palladio dedicated some words concerning the garden in his treatise. The interiors of the villa's piano nobile were frescoed by Paolo Veronese between 1560 and 1562, according to a complex and erudite iconographic program, presumably suggested by Daniele Barbaro himself.

The central theme is that of the Harmony and Peace, that lie above and watch over the family, the work in the fields, the affairs of state, and the universe as a whole. The walls of the dwelling are brought to life by allegorical, mythological, astrological, and religious images that merge in a continuous sequence of cross-references from one room to another. Veronese skillfully adapts the painted architecture to the rooms and the spaces inside, thus creating a clever effect involving the perspectival alternation between real and frescoed architecture. Palladio's simple and well-proportioned spaces are transformed into lively and joyous environments that open onto landscapes for as far as the eye can see, fading into the infinite, in the niches animated by allegorical figures and in the doors left ajar, so that life-size figures can peer out. Overhead, on the ceilings, is a bright sky streaked with light clouds seated upon which are gods that by appearing before humans almost seem to want to get closer to them, shortening the distances between their two worlds. Beyond the faux balustrades, the view stretches over bucolic scenarios inhabited by palaces and classic ruins, where mythological settings and visions of the surrounding countryside come together and seemingly disrupt the sense of real time. One's thoughts are inevitably invited to turn toward the past, antiquity, classical culture, the same culture as that of the owners of the house: Daniele and Marcantonio Barbaro who, in a space that seems to become lost in the surrounding nature, celebrated their culture, the prosperity of their lands and their family. Scenes and landscapes are framed in the marvelous and illusionistic architecture whose rules Veronese knew well, demonstrating this in his creation of a perfect fiction. In some of the rooms he pierces the ceiling to make room for arbors with climbing vines. He adapts his architectures to the size of the rooms, and the optical illusion can be seen from any point of view, but especially from the middle of the room. The unique-

Ceiling of the Sala
dell'Olimpo

In the midst of the frescoes in the Sala a Crociera, a page peers out from a door offering his welcome

On the opposite wall, a little girl looks out from another door with an expression of curiosity on her face

View of the Sala dell'Olimpo and in the background the nymphaeum

ness of these frescoes does not so much lie in the themes dealt with, since the depictions of planets, divine banquets, seasons or allusions to the virtues and family life of the owners were customary from the fifteenth century. Their specific characteristic concerns the way the subjects are portrayed and how they adapt to the rooms, where reality and fiction come together to create solid harmony.

In such an important overlapping between the space designed by Palladio and the illusionistic space realized by Veronese, some scholars have noticed a sort of conflict between the two artists. The dispute seems to have been corroborated by the fact that Palladio, in his *Four Books*, in describing the plan for Villa Maser, forgot to mention Veronese's frescoes, something he had instead done when discussing other villas, where the author of the paintings was referred to. It is more likely that the architect, as if intimidated by the strong personality of his patrons who also influenced Veronese's work, had cut out a role for himself as the general coordinator of the works. Proof of this lies in the fact that the two artists met again in the refectory of the convent of San Giorgio, where Veronese would paint the *Wedding at Cana*. Nor did the relationship with the Barbaro end after Maser. Indeed, Marcantonio continued to support Palladio's later Venetian projects, and in 1580, after his brother passed away, he summoned him to Maser once again, this time to design a small temple pertinent to the villa, but that would also serve as the parish church for the hamlet of Maser. The architect experimented with and studied the classical model based on a central plan, while keeping one eye on the Roman Pantheon. This was Palladio's very last work. Soon afterwards he would die in Maser, without ever seeing it finished.

On the previous spread
View of the nymphaeum

The *barchesse*
of the villa end with
two dovecotes, topped
by a tympanum below
which is a meridian

View of the garden
toward the landscape.
Thanks to an ingenious
hydraulic system,
the water, after
it has been used inside
the villa, is channeled
toward the garden in
the fountain of Neptune,
visible at the rear,
and from there it flows
into the fields

Temple of Villa Barbaro,
view from outside

Semicircular exedra with
the fountain of Neptune

**On the following
spread**
Bird's eye view of the
complex of Villa Barbaro
in Maser

In the fourteenth century Cangrande della Scala expanded the city of Verona by having a new circle of walls built beyond the right bank of the Adige River. Over the years, representatives of the merchant and artisanal classes had settled in this area, most of whom were millers, tanners, and weavers, who were drawn by the possibility of exploiting the water of the nearby river for their activities.

VERONA

The Giusti Garden

On the previous spread
The cypress-lined
path at the entrance
to the garden

In the early fifteenth century, Provolo

Giusti, a Florentine wool carder, settled in this area on an estate that was part vineyard and part vegetable garden at the foot of a slight slope. The space was ample and airy, protected and sunlit, and in it he set up two dye-works with stretchers where he could hang cloth. As its economic situation improved, the family's social prestige grew as well, and it began to hold evermore important positions in the city government.

Slowly, the original, profitable wool-making activity was abandoned in favor of legal, diplomatic, and political activities that allowed the Giusti to expand their estate, purchasing land and properties in the city and county. Palazzo Giusti dates to the sixteenth century and is laid out according to an irregular plan, the result of the union of a series of buildings that were acquired over time by the mid-fifteenth century and then later joined in a single front.

The outer facade was embellished with decorations that are now only partially visible: a series of Doric columns alternated with windows stretching all along the facade, and at the attic level was a frieze featuring images of military and musical instruments with triglyphs in between. The facade was completed with images of the allegories of Faith, Hope, Charity, and Justice. The building featured a mezzanine, piano nobile, and a third floor, the attic, which was occupied and used by the servants. To either side of the entrance two stairways were decorated with statues leading up to the piano nobile, where one of the most interesting rooms was filled with mirrors. This is known as the Triumph of Aurora room, painted by Francesco Lorenzi, a pupil of Giambattista Tiepolo. At the center of the ceiling was the *Triumph of Aurora*, while the scenes along the walls told the story of the preparation of Aurora, her awakening, Apollo dissipating the darkness, the hours yoking the horses of the Chariot of the Sun. The room also contained six monochrome allegorical compositions representing Music, Science, Plenty, Nobility, Friendship, and Merit. Count Agostino Giusti was responsible for making improvements to the palazzo in the sixteenth century. Giusti was a highly cultivated figure, a knight of the Republic of Venice, and a gentleman of the Grand Duke of Tuscany. In 1583, after solving a series of issues concerning patrimony and inheritance, the count officially became the owner of the estate.

The meadows where woolen cloth was at one time hung were replaced by a flat garden closed off on all four sides and separated by

View of the palazzo

The palazzo seen from
the cypress-lined path

THE GIUSTI GARDEN

Francesco Lorenzi,
The Triumph of Aurora

View of the Sala
degli Specchi
or of *The Triumph
of Aurora*

a path in the middle lined with cypresses, in axis with the entrance
to the palazzo. To either side of the path were geometric flower-beds
and a fish pond with an island at the center—which was later placed
underground—that could be accessed by a staircase topped by an
arbor. There was also a labyrinth with boxwood hedges, redesigned in
1786 by the architect Luigi Trezza after the previous sixteenth-century model. However, the garden did not end with this regularly divided
quadrangle, as the spirit of the time believed it should. It continued
beyond: the level surface suddenly became a steep cliff about ten meters high, at the top of which the land again stretched gently as far as
the edge of the property, close to the ancient Scaliger walls.

The problem of the unevenness could be solved by creating a series
of terraces modeled after Roman gardens; after all, examples—from
the Cortile del Belvedere to Villa d'Este—were not lacking. Confirmed
here instead was the Venetian tradition of the spontaneous garden,
immersed in the landscape and in constant conversation with it. And
all this did was accentuate the diversity between the two portions, one
ordered, the other wild, arousing a sense of unease, of looming dan-

The stairway leading up to the piano nobile is filled with statues

ger, further accentuated by the presence of a stone mascaron with a sinister expression that hung threateningly, almost defying the force of gravity.

The feeling of angst that it aroused is masterfully described in a precious record from that period, the *Sileno, ovvero delle bellezze del luogo dell'illustrissimo signor conte Giovanni Giusti*, a pamphlet written in 1620 by Francesco Poma, a physician and botany enthusiast, as well as a friend of the family. In it, the erudite scholar describes an imaginary dialog between a "familiar citizen" (i.e. Poma himself), and a "stranger," where the former tells the latter about the beauties of the home and garden, providing a rather meticulous description. In time this writing has also proven to be a rather useful tool in seeking to achieve a more in-depth understanding of its structure and meaning. As they stroll along, the citizen cannot help but point out to his guest the extent to which the profusion of flowers, fruit, and colors that are dominant all around them restores that idea of eternal spring and paradise that only the garden can offer, but that is suddenly upset by the vision of the rock formation looming over them, causing them to experience a sense of loss and fear. Hence, the garden does not just arouse a feeling of certainty and serenity, but uncertainty and fright before the mystery of nature and human life itself, in which feelings both good and evil occur in turn. Contradictory sentiments that would only be solved by reaching the final destination, the objective: the circular temple symbolizing cosmic perfection, serenity, and harmony, located up high, in an isolated position. Although the temple no longer exists, it can be seen in the images from that period. The image that it conveys is no longer that of the Renaissance man who governs the world by scientific rules, mathematics, and geometry; rather, it is that of a fragile man who, as the Renaissance was coming to an end, had lost his sense of certainty, and expressed through the garden all the weight of his restless life as he entered the tormented and deeply anxious world of Mannerism.

However, there is also another theme that is introduced by the vision of the garden: it is that of the relationship between art and nature, reality and fiction, which is reflected in the settings of some of the grottos at the end of the path of cypresses, excavated at the bottom of the cliff.

The grotto, whether natural or artificial, after the model of the ones existing in Roman villas, was recommended by Leon Battista Alberti,

Jupiter names Diana goddess of hunting. The fresco decorates the ceiling of one of the rooms in the eastern wing of the palazzo

who also suggested the type of material that should be used to make it. The image of the grotto, which appeared in the garden over the course of the sixteenth century, evoked the image of an inaccessible and secret world. Venturing inside it was like entering the bowels of the earth, a place where the concept of time, deprived of the sun crossing the sky, was erased, replaced by the time of the soul.

The most unique and odd site was that of the Grotta degli Specchi, which was in a central position, at the very end of the avenue of cypresses. The grotto, which still exists today without the decorations that once adorned it, was painstakingly described by Heinrich Schickhardt, the official architect of Frederick I of Württemberg, who traveled to Italy to study between 1598 and 1600. Schickhardt visited the garden in 1598, and wrote an interesting description of it accompanied by a drawing in his travel notebook.

On the wall at the back, to either side of a central niche, there were

once two large mirrors, each of which divided into sixteen squares, alluding to the idea of two grates that opened onto the garden. The side walls were decorated with paintings that simulated a loggia overlooking the landscape. Entering the grotto, Schickhardt wrote, was like entering an open space overlooking yet another garden. All this was made possible thanks to the clever play of mirrors and reflections that combined the view of the real garden, the one behind the visitor, and the illusionistic landscape of the loggias. The visitor was illuded into thinking he or she was entering an open setting, and not a dark grotto as they might have expected. The sources also say the grotto was lined with mother-of-pearl, corals, shells, stones, and colored stones akin to the ancient models.

In the northwestern part of the garden, just past the greenhouses is another grotto, known as the Grotta dell'Eco, a sort of cave dug into the rock featuring an octagonal plan with four perpendicular arms arranged in the manner of a Greek cross.

The structure was designed so that its acoustics would be good, as concerts were likely held there. It is unknown whether the structure dates to the late sixteenth century, as the sources from that period do not mention it, while it is recalled by numerous visitors who over the course of the eighteenth century went to admire the garden. After all, Agostino Giusti's love of music was well known. A room on the ground floor of the palazzo was reserved for the Accademia dei Filarmonici, the famous musical institution founded in 1543, one of the oldest in Europe, and headquartered in the Palazzo Giusti from 1565 to 1583. Agostino himself had been its president since 1581, the year when Torquato Tasso's *Aminta* was performed in the garden. This was followed by numerous other open-air performances.

Having gone past the Grotta dell'Eco, continuing eastward, one finds another cavity, which was probably used to shelter the plants in winter. Continuing along in the same direction is a chapel with a rectangular plan, it too excavated directly into the rock, where religious functions were once held. Rising up to one side of the chapel is a turret from which a set of steps leads to the upper garden. At one time, according to Poma's testimony, there was an orchard here.

Agostino Giusti was a man of great erudition, and he adorned his garden with ancient findings, statues, busts, sarcophagi, and Roman epigraphs, some of which are still visible, for one of the rare private epigraphic and antiquarian collections existing today.

THE GIUSTI GARDEN

Bird's eye view of the
garden with boxwood
compartments and
a maze redesigned
in the 18th century,
after the previous
16th-century model

The grotesque
mascaron above the
Grotta degli Specchi

Interior of the Grotta
degli Specchi. The side
walls were decorated
with frescoes. Located
on the wall at the rear
were mirrors that
reflected the garden
behind the visitor,
thereby creating the
illusion of entering
another green space

**On the following
spread**
View of the garden
toward the palazzo

The history of the Villa Imperiale in Pesaro is closely linked to the political events that over the course of the Renaissance ravaged Italy, which was divided into small States, and refined and elegant courts brimming with art and culture coveted by the great European monarchies, but also by the country's own dukes, lords, and popes who had ambitious plans to gain power and conquer.

PESARO

Villa Imperiale

On the previous spread
View of the Villa
Imperiale, in the
foreground the original
Sforza's villa

Toward the mid-fifteenth century, precisely

in 1452, Alessandro Sforza, Lord of Pesaro, and his brother France-sco, Duke of Milan, decided to build a villa not far from Pesaro, on the slopes of Mount San Bartolo: a quadrangular building featuring a tall tower in the area corresponding to the main entrance and with a porticoed side overlooking the valley, probably a hunting lodge used for defensive purposes. Tradition would have it that the name of the residence was a tribute to Emperor Frederick III of Habsburg who, as a guest in the city of Pesaro in 1452, was invited to lay the first stone. The dwelling was abandoned in the early sixteenth century, when the ruthless Cesare Borgia, with the support of Pope Alexander VI, his putative father, succeeded in creating a unitary state in Central Italy by expelling the various seigneurs, including the Sforza.

In the sights of the perfidious commander was the duchy of Urbino as well, where Guidobaldo I, the son of Federico da Montefeltro, was in power, and managed to flee to Venice.

Guidobaldo, who had no heirs, had designated his sister's son, Francesco Maria I della Rovere as his successor. Francesco Maria was the descendant of a noble family originally from Savona, as well as being the nephew of Sixtus IV, who, upon being elected pope in 1471, had tried to bring honor to the family by facilitating his nephew's social ascent. When Alexander VI died and was replaced by Pope Julius della Rovere, the duchy of Urbino was handed back to its legitimate owners, and, in 1513, Francesco Maria I was also given the seigneury of Pesaro. Once again, however, fate was against him, and after just three years the new pope, Leo X de' Medici, forced Francesco Maria into exile in favor of his nephew, Lorenzo. The duke, who in the meantime had been joined in marriage with Eleonora Gonzaga, retired with his wife to Mantua. The Lord of Pesaro would not let matters go, however, and in 1517, thanks also to the help of his mother-in-law, Isabella d'Este, he assembled a makeshift army and set out for the papal region, where he intended to take back what had been stolen from him. On his own, with very few means, but with the population on his side, he managed to withstand the papal troops for about eight months, and to win the bitter battle that raged around the Villa Imperiale and, we are told, even right inside it. Though the duchy was reconquered, Francesco did not get it back until 1521, thanks to the support of the new pope, Hadrian VI.

Putto in the Sala dei
Semibusti attributed
to Bronzino

The connection
between the old villa
and the new one

VILLA IMPERIALE

Ceiling of the Sala
delle Cariatidi
representing the battle
won by Francesco Maria
della Rovere
to reconquer the duchy

View of the Sala
delle Cariatidi

Once Francesco had gotten back his property, he devoted himself to renewing the city of Pesaro, which became the new political and economic center of the duchy because it was closer to the sea than Urbino. Francesco did not have a lot of time on his hands, having in the meantime been nominated by the city of Venice governor of its army. This meant he had to be in the Serenissima most of the time. Francesco chose to improve the city's defenses by having new fortifications built and by refurbishing and remodeling the old Sforza buildings, including the Palazzo Ducale in the city and the Villa Imperiale. The works were commissioned from Gerolamo Genga, a native of Urbino as well as being a painter, scenographer, and architect. The artist had begun his activity in the workshop of Luca Signorelli during the same years that Raphael was there. He had then gone on to study under Perugino, and, upon his master's death, had

Sala degli Amorini, detail

Sala delle Fatiche
d'Ercole, detail

Sala degli Amorini

returned to Urbino to the court of Guidobaldo I, for whom had made some decorative scenes. After the dukes were exiled, he had gone to Florence and Siena. In 1519, he was in Rome, where he made a *Resurrection* for the banker Agostino Chigi, and where he could also study the ancient monuments and the buildings of Bramante and Raphael. In 1522, Francesco Maria I della Rovere summoned Genga to Pesaro, where he named him court artist and, among his other tasks, assigned him the job of refurbishing and expanding the old Villa Imperiale that had been built by Alessandro Sforza. The building must have been in very poor condition, especially after the battle that had taken place in 1517, and it was certainly not suited to the rank of its owners and their court.

Genga reorganized the interiors making them more functional and spacious: he rearranged the ground floor so that it could be used for the various services, while on the piano nobile he created a series of formal and reception rooms: there were nine in all, eight of which splendidly frescoed. Efforts to decorate the interiors began in 1529, once the remodeling work had been completed, and they were made by an excellent group of artists coordinated by Genga, which included such names as Bronzino, Dosso Dossi and Raffaellino del Colle.

The theme of the frescoes, with their evident celebratory purpose, was suggested by the duke, and recalled the most important events in his life: the oath-taking of the troops he had assembled to free his duchy, his military investitures, his victory upon regaining the duchy, and his participation in the crowning of Charles V. The historical scenes occupy the vault of the ceiling in every room and are framed in precious ornamentation or faux tapestries held up by putti. On the walls of the rooms are fantastic architectures and landscapes further valorized by tales from mythology, grotesques, and mascarons. Gerolamo Genga expressed all his skill as a scenographer by knocking down the facades of the walls and creating open galleries that overlooked from above the landscapes unfolding homogeneously along all four walls, and further enhancing the optical illusion in an elegant play of cross-references between reality and fiction.

The cycle of frescoes with the heraldry devices of Francesco Maria I ends in the room known as "della Calunnia" (Room of Slander), representing the scene recounted by the Greek poet Lucian of Samosata, a scene that was also handled by Leon Battista Alberti in his architecture treatise *De re aedificatoria:* Midas, the famous king with donkey ears, the bad judge, sits on his throne poorly advised and surrounded by the personification of the vices, while far away, all alone, *nuda Veritas* appears in the guise of a disrobed maiden who points to the heavens as the only source of justice. The reference to the duke's personal experiences, to his enemies' evil and avarice, is evident. In the end, however, truth and justice triumph, and on the opposite wall is an image of the duke kneeling, finally crowned by glory.

At the same time that the old building was being refurbished, it was decided that the complex should be expanded by adding another wing to it, the so-called Imperiale Nuova. In spite of the fact that the two parts of the villa were made at different times, the whole has proven to be cohesive and undivided, as if the two parts had originated from the same one project.

The new building was constructed against the slope of San Bartolo hill, and was connected to the old building by an arch supporting a hanging corridor. Genga solved the problem of the uneven ground by creating a rectangular system consisting of three sloping terraces, after the model of Bramante's Belvedere, albeit more modest in size. Starting from the top, the first terrace hosts a large garden set on a hilltop; the second level has a smaller hanging garden; the third one contains a sunken courtyard overlooked by a tall residential building.

The courtyard is located at the level of the Villa Nuova's piano nobile; below it there are rooms for amenities. The complex, formed

Small hallway decorated with caryatids. Top, in the medallion, the image of Peace burning weapons

VILLA IMPERIALE

Nuda Veritas, detail of the Sala della Calunnia

Central scene of the *Allegory of Calumny* in the eponymous room. King Midas, with his donkey ears, surrounded by the personifications of the vices

On the previous spread
The Sala Grande.
The ceiling is decorated in *papier-mâché* and visible in the coffers are the initials of the Dukes of Montefeltro

by the sequence of the two gardens, the central courtyard, and the building, is contained on either side by two narrow buildings for the staircases and foyers. The gardens and the courtyard are separated by rather tall walls, and from the lower level of the courtyard one cannot see, nor can one imagine, the way the upper terraces develop upwards.

A broader vision of the whole is obtained from the top of the garden, where the view of the valley is truly unique. The top of the villa and of the side buildings connecting the gardens were transformed into terraces bordered by balustrades, a sort of "hanging" walk along the entire surface of the Villa Nuova.

The Villa Imperiale Nuova is a curious dwelling. It was conceived as a closed organism, with very few openings to the outside, and what would seem to be the facade is actually deprived of an entrance. Access is through the Villa Vecchia: after crossing all the reception areas, which describe the duke's virtues, one reaches the hanging corridor and enters the Ala Nuova (New Wing). Here the closed spaces used as residences occupy a small part of the structure; they are mostly located on the piano nobile overlooking the courtyard, and include the dukes' summer apartments separated by an open room facing the inner courtyard across a loggia. Another entrance described in the sources is located above, in a passageway that goes from the wood to the last garden. Not just the entrance, but the interior paths also appear complicated. The stairways follow an intricate network of patterns and connections separating the traditional itineraries related to the life of the court from the more rapid and functional ones of the servants. Each level, from the cellars to the terraces, can be reached quickly without ever running into any of the villa's guests, thanks to a system of spiral staircases that are a truly surprising architectural element.

In a scenic decoration such as this one, there had to be gardens as well, which were especially loved by Eleonora Gonzaga. A drawing from that period shows the rectangular courtyard with a statue in the middle, while a subsequent eighteenth-century relief depicts a parterre with three fountains. The two to the side were no doubt basins in which water was collected and then used for irrigation. Furthermore, since the sixteenth century there has been proof of the existence of a grotto, water features, and fountains set in motion by a complex hydraulic action. Genga, after all, had planned a

sophisticated system to collect and distribute the water as far as the garden highest up.

Growing in the two hanging gardens were numerous species of citrus fruits, citrons, lemons, but especially sour oranges. In the lower terrace the citruses were once cultivated on an espalier along a retaining wall, while in the flower-beds they were arranged in a regular pattern, with sections of myrtle plants and bay trees dotted with lemons, citrons, and hybrids known as *bizzarrie* (oddities), all of which came from Savona. It seems that the upper garden, it too decorated with espaliers of citrus plants, on the corners of the upper side featured a sort of loggia, consisting of two large, closed exedrae used to store citrus fruit in the winter season. In the summer, instead, they could be used as open pavilions, places where one could stop and converse.

The records also describe the existence of vines that were probably meant to offer shade to the paths in the terraces. The upper part of the complex thus resembled a sort of green architecture, a natural wall that merged with the green of the wood all around, which, at the same time, lent itself to comparison and conversation with the architecturally defined building—one that was vaguely reminiscent of antiquity—just opposite it.

The Villa Imperiale Nuova was mostly used for leisure activities and *otium*, meaning distraction and relief from military activity. The villa's function was determined in two inscriptions placed, respectively, on the facade and on the trabeation of the inner courtyard, and were written by Cardinal Pietro Bembo, an erudite man of letters and renowned humanist, highly esteemed in sixteenth-century cultural spheres. The dedication by Eleonora to her husband is as follows: "To Francesco Maria, Duke of the Metaurenses, a war veteran, for whom his wife Leonora had this villa built for his delight"; the second inscription continues as follows: "so that—to compensate for the sun, the dust, the sleepless nights, the hard work—military activity alternated with rest can procure great glory and better results." The construction, as we mentioned before, is complex with respect to the former, as well as being atypical, the result of its inventor's work with scenography and theater, an artist who, in creating such a complex maze of corridors, staircases, junctions, and blind entrances seems to have also been inspired by military architecture.

The link with the theater is evident in the lower courtyard, closed off within four cleverly decorated walls featuring apertures, niches,

The southern facade
of the inner courtyard
and the hanging garden

The loggia
of the courtyard
entrance

**On the following
spread**
View of the southern
facade of the
courtyard, the
hanging garden,
and the upper
garden

pilasters, cornices and overhangs, constantly alternating between fulls and voids, a sort of stage curtain with perfect acoustics, to the point of considering this to be a suitable place for parties and performances. Although no records have been found telling us that the courtyard was used for plays, this space has the same purpose as the rest of the villa: it is a place used for parties and leisure activities; a placed closed unto itself, and far from wars and perils. However, it is also a place of representation, the manifestation of power rediscovered by the Della Rovere. A villa that should reflect the culture worthy of a nephew of the pope, namely Francesco Maria Della Rovere, a noble commander who, legend has it, had the honor of being portrayed when he was still young in the *School of Athens*, one of the most famous frescoes painted by Raphael, he too, like Genga, a native of Urbino.

In Bomarzo the geometry of the Renaissance garden, with its straight paths and regular, symmetrical, and carefully trimmed hedges, vanishes to make way for the unkempt nature of a wood where singular apparitions manifest themselves: giants fighting, fluvial and marine deities, frightening, charming, or bizarre figures that bring the landscape to life acting as the custodians of a message that has never been revealed.

Sacred Wood

The theater area
represents the final
destination
of Poliphilo's path

The leaning house

**On the following
spread**
The image of Glory,
quick, unstable,
and uncontrollable
(the sphere) on the back
of a slow tortoise
is a warning in favor
of hastiness, careful
to be prudent at the
same time

The artificer of a wonder of this kind was

Pier Francesco, otherwise known as Vicino Orsini, the grand-nephew
of Leo X, who chose to follow a military career and also had literary
interests. In 1545, Orsini married Giulia Farnese, a relative of the
cardinal, consolidating the family's relations with the Farnese and
benefiting from his privileged relationship with the pope's family.
Vicino devoted himself to a military career for about twelve years,
gravitating in the orbit of Rome. He was sent to Germany to aid
Charles V in the struggle against the Protestant princes. Later, he
went to France, and then to Flanders, where he was imprisoned for
two years, and released in 1555. The following year he was again at
the pope's side to oppose the troops of the Duke of Alba, Fernando
Álvarez de Toledo, and witness the destruction of Montefortino ordered by the pope. The inhabitants of the hamlet, along with their
lord, a member of the Colonna family, had gone over to the Spanish
side, and besieged a commando of one hundred foot-soldiers who had
been sent under orders by Vicino himself. The pope's reaction was
swift and ruthless, and the hamlet was put to the fire and the sword.

Even the women and children were murdered. According to some
scholars it was this dramatic episode that led Vicino to abandon his
military career. For a few years he continued to hold political-diplo-
matic roles, but after the Peace of Cateau-Cambrésis, in 1559, he
permanently retired to Bomarzo, where he dedicated himself to his
studies, literature, and the garden. He also worked on completing
the Palazzo Orsini. The family residence was made up of several sections, which were the result of restorations and remodeling that were
conducted over time. Giovanni Corrado Orsini, Vicino's father, decided to transform the pre-existing medieval castle into a residential
palace on the occasion of his marriage to Clarice Orsini, his second
wife. In 1519, he drafted an agreement with the Siena architect Baldassarre Peruzzi who designed the building, as demonstrated in the
pen sketch of the palazzo rediscovered in a drawing preserved at the
Uffizi. Although the construction of the building occurred in several
stages and with numerous changes along the way, Peruzzi's work is
still visible in some of the architectural elements, such as the windows on the piano nobile in the shape of aedicula with acroterions, or
the entrance portal. The southern wing of the palazzo, also conceived
by Peruzzi, was finished by Vicino, who had it connected to the old
medieval structures. He added moral and allegorical inscriptions to

this part of the building in order to prepare those who were about to visit the garden, foreshadowing some of the themes that would be portrayed in the figures sculpted in the blocks of peperino emerging from the vegetation. The figurative elements in the garden were in fact conceived directly on site, characterized by the presence of numerous stone blocks in which Vicino created his subjects directly, inspired by Michelangelo's poetics of the "non-finito."

Esteemed and accredited scholars have analyzed and examined the sculptures that animate this fantastic wood as a whole, seeking to decipher the secret message expressed therein. No doubt the complex was meant to be a sort of eighth wonder of the world, a concept that is conveyed in some of the stones scattered throughout the garden. One of them reads: "CHI CON CIGLIA INARCATE / E LABRA STRETTE / NON VA PER QUESTO LOCO / MANCO AMMIRA / LE FAMOSE DEL MONDO / MOLI SETTE." The inscription accompanies one of the two sphinxes that gaze at each other from a short distance and welcome the visitor at the entrance, foreshadowing the journey they are about to take in a sort of garden of wonders, where reality makes way for a world upside down that becomes lost beyond space and beyond time. A downwards path unwinds amidst the fronds of pubescent oaks, Adriatic oaks, manna ashes and shrubs from which giant figures and bizarre architecture that have an estranging effect appear. Images bor-

The colossal statue of a woman with two serpent's tails recalling the image of a mermaid could allude to the seductive and frightening spells that any wise man must be capable of fleeing from

rowed from scenography made for the theater and festivities, without overlooking the literary sources the garden is inspired by: numerous and heterogenous, they interweave and overlap with each other, creating complex contents that are hard to read and interpret. Just as it is generally believed that the founding date is 1552, as recorded on an epigraph inside, it is also certain that Vicino devoted to the wood his entire life, and that, consequently, new themes or additions accompanied and in some cases were juxtaposed with the previous ones, thus enriching the pattern of meanings. An early inspiration for the garden's composition can be found in the *Hypnerotomachia Poliphili*, a book attributed to Francesco Colonna, and highly popular during the course of the Renaissance. It is a prose work that describes the young Poliphilo's "dream of the battle of love." It tells of the journey through fantastic architectures, splendid gardens, antiquity, Roman ruins, obelisks and epigraphs, he takes in search of his beloved Polia, whom he eventually finds, only to lose her again upon awakening. It is an esoteric course brimming with allegorical references and complex meanings, a compendium of the most up-to-date principles of philosophy and of Renaissance philology. Vicino's park, like Colonna's dream, was devoted to the woman he loved and had lost. One year after he had retired to private life, Vicino suffered a bad blow when his wife, with whom he was very close, died. In honor of Giulia, to whom

L'ANTRO LA FONTE IL L[...]
D'OGNI OSCVRO PENSIER GL[...]   M

The cavern
of the Nymphs

the garden had been devoted from the start, he had a temple built at the top of a slope, at the highest point of the path. The funerary nature of the monument is clear to see in the boundary stones featuring skulls and crossbones arranged at the corners of the building. There are numerous similarities and analogies between this building and the architectures described in the *Hypnerotomachia*, starting from the temple dedicated to Venus, "giver of life," where Polia appears before the young man. It is likely that in Bomarzo the starting point of the visitors path, before the garden was expanded with other sculptures, was precisely the temple at the top of the knoll. Poliphilo's destination is "the island of Cythera," where the garden of Venus can be found, represented by Vicino in the area that joins the theater, the herms, and the sacrarium of Aphrodite, the place of everlasting love that survives even death. The path to reach it is scattered with images such as the fountain of Pegasus, a faux ruin, and a nymphaeum with the three Graces, all of which inspired by the *Hypnerotomachia*.

However, Bomarzo is more than this, and as mentioned before, the many themes here are interwoven. The first original design was followed by a second one conceived after 1565, when the sculptures assumed colossal shapes and the literary texts of reference changed genre. The repertoire now came from chivalric literature, in which one of the favorite topics is that of the wood as a place of enchantment

Not far from
the nymphaeum
is the statue of Venus
on a basement that has
the features of a flying
monster with wings
in the shape
of a half-shell,
the attribute of the
goddess of love

The image of an
elephant carrying
a Roman legionary could
allude to the battle
of the Christians against
the Saracens that is told
in *Jerusalem Delivered*,
and therefore to the
Battle of Lepanto where,
among other things, one
of Vicino Orsini's sons,
Orazio, had lost his life.
The sculptural group
could thus be a bizarre
tribute to his memory

and sorcery. The knight had to be able to make his way through the thick vegetation and head down tangled paths. Along the way he had to undergo a series of trials: he had to slay dragons, fight giants, face sorcery and spells, resist the temptations that he encountered along the way. Seen in this light, the sculptures of Bomarzo might allude to the various trials faced by the knight along a crooked and unpredictable path, at the end of which, once he had reached the top, victory and fame awaited him. Hence, the temple of Giulia assumes the image of the Temple of Victory, Glory, and Virtue.

In the world of *Orlando furioso* by Ludovico Ariosto, passions and sentiments accompany magic and fear, and act as a backdrop to the adventures of the famous knight. On the other side of a wood, Orlando, as he spasmodically searched for Angelica, would find the place where she had been with Medoro, and where she had left traces of the new love that had brought them together. Orlando, who feels betrayed, is overwhelmed by the madness that clouds his mind, and after ripping out all the trees in a forest ends up killing an unwitting shepherd, tearing him from limb to limb. The image of that madness can be found in Vicino's wood specifically in the statue evoking Orlando's attack of his unfortunate victim. Perhaps it is a warning that one should not exceed in his passions, or an acknowledgment that madness can overcome reason even for just a moment. It is further proof that the wood, with its bizarre representations, is far-removed from the rules of the Renaissance garden, overturning the established formulae there; detachment that can also be seen in the slanted house, where the geometric and mathematical canons that build up the perfect Renaissance space are used for the opposite intent, that of disorienting. The tilted walls and floors produce the feeling of losing one's balance, and consequently, any sense of reality. Vicino was a man of war who, in the second half of his life, chose to isolate himself from the world so he could devote himself to study. Other figures lost in the wood recall Ariosto's poem: the sea monster, which can either refer to the liberation of Angelica or to the whale on which Astolfo reaches the island of Alcina; the image of Pegasus, which might allude to Orlando's hippogriff; and there is also a giant tortoise with a female figure riding it. The latter refers to another literary work, Luigi Pulci's *Morgante*, and to the episode in which Morgante kills a gigantic tortoise that resembles a mountain and then eats it in the company of his eccentric squire Margette.

Chivalric literature provided Orsini with a way to recall the events

The statue of Glaucus is located at the end of the path. On the monster's head is a globe topped by a castle, the image of the Orsini family. There are some who say the statue could allude to the changing fate that the family, however powerful it may have been, had to take into account

The statue of a bear holds the Orsini family coat of arms

of his military past, poised between irony and a sense of disquiet. Bomarzo is a garden in which humans can become lost, where nature is not dominant; it is a tangle of paths that lead to bewilderment, fear, or salvation. There have been numerous interpretations of the garden over time: an initiatory path, an alchemical one, a path aimed at spiritual growth along which man abandons his original brutality; or perhaps it is the representation on Earth of the celestial sphere with the stars and the constellations, envisioning the celebration of the noble origins of the Orsini family in the Ursa Minor constellation.

Over the centuries, time and negligence worked together, helping the forest to grow and conceal the wonders there from the eyes of many, until, almost by chance, Bomarzo re-emerged from oblivion in the early 1900s. The studies began in the 1940s when artists and literati rediscovered the magical world of the Orsini. First among all of them was Salvador Dalí, who was bewitched by a place where abstract surrealism seemed to come to life in surprising forms. Having re-emerged from oblivion and been brought back to history thanks also to the care of its recent owners, and the restoration work undertaken, the park has never stopped fascinating contemporary artists. Its shapes have appeared in the most varied of places, such as in Parc Güell in Barcelona, or in the colored and eccentric works of Niki de Saint Phalle in the Tarot Garden. Whatever the case may be, in the past Bomarzo must have been even more luxuriant than it is today. Sources describe it as an extraordinary place, with water features and fish ponds of which only a few traces remain today. An idea of just how enchanting the place was can be found in the drawings of the gardens of wonders from the late sixteenth century that Giovanni Guerra made for Cardinal Pietro Aldobrandini. Nineteenth-century records instead say that the original garden was not only inhabited by figures inspired directly by the rock formations, but also by sculptures placed there deliberately. Testimony that could also be confirmed by a new drawing by Giovanni Guerra, which portrays, around the fountain of Pegasus, the nine Muses along with statues of Apollo, Zeus, Mercury, and Bacchus. These statues were presumably stolen, seeing they could easily be transported, unlike the huge masses of carved rock that, anchored to the ground, have remained there, the mute actors of a vast open-air theater created for the purpose of surprising, astonishing, and even disturbing the viewer, a foreshadowing of the Baroque poetics that was soon to spread throughout the gardens of Europe.

Vignanello rises up on a dark, elongated spur of tufaceous rock, where a community of Benedictines settled in 835. Over the centuries, a series of events saw this fortress, that was fought over, change hands, from aristocratic families to religious institutions, until 1531, when Pope Clement VII perpetually granted the fief of Vignanello to Beatrice Farnese, the wife of Antonio Baglioni and the niece of Cardinal Alessandro Farnese, who in a few years' time would be elected to the papacy as Pope Paul III.

VIGNANELLO

Ruspoli Castle

On the previous spread
The castle and the
garden of Vignanello.
In the foreground the
central fountain, also
known as the fish pond

The transformation of the ancient

fortress into a castle took place in the early 1530s. The castle featured a rectangular plan, and was flanked at the corners by four towers with scarp walls and surrounded by a moat. A drawbridge could be used to access the residence. Ortensia, Beatrice's daughter, married Sforza Vicino Marescotti, the scion of a noble Bolognese family that, legend has it, descended from Marius Scotus, a Scottish mercenary and commander at the service of Charlemagne. Marius Scotus' family later settled in Bologna, where it was one of the city's most influential clans. Work to refurbish the original fortress, which had been built by monks, was probably initiated by Beatrice and was continued after her death by Ortensia and Sforza Vicino. In 1536, Pope Paul III confirmed the investiture for the two spouses at Vignanello Castle, perpetually granting them countship.

Count Sforza was a violent man who was easily enraged. According to legend, it was the countess who murdered him with a poker in one of the rooms on the piano nobile. After her husband died, Ortensia remarried twice, and again both husbands died in mysterious circumstances. But each time that Ortensia was jailed and tried for her husband's death, she was found innocent and allowed to go back to govern her properties, which in the meantime had grown thanks to what she inherited through marriage. But that is not all. Ortensia did not just get rid of her three husbands. It seems she used various kinds of poison to kill off four of her six children, so that only her firstborn, Alfonso, would be the heir to her property, which would otherwise have been broken up. In 1574, Marcantonio, Alfonso's son, married Ottavia, the daughter of Vicino Orsini, the famous owner and inventor of the Garden of Bomarzo. The atmosphere at Vignanello, however, was not especially peaceful, not just because of Marcantonio's deep scorn for his father's authority, but also because of the continuous fighting between the counts and the inhabitants there, who were constantly being burdened by the arrogance, violence, and insolence of the despotic owners. Concerned about his daughter's fate, Vicino managed to get Pope Gregory XIII to confiscate the fief from the two aristocrats, ordering their arrest and that they be thrown into the prison of Tor di Nona, in Rome. Thanks to the intercession of the pope, Alfonso was able to avoid the death penalty, but not the confiscation of his estate, which meant that he could never return to Vignanello.

Notwithstanding the many problems and the unpleasant events

View of the secret
garden, arranged
at a lower level

Entrance to the garden

View of the room where,
according to legend,
Ortensia Farnese
Marescotti murdered
her first husband.
The Marescotti family
coat of arms was
removed from the
fireplace that featured
the double emblems
of the spouses, leaving
only that of the Farnese

View of the Sala
del Camino with
the coat of arms
of the Marescotti
removed

that upset the hamlet, Alfonso had still been able to initiate several important projects in the fortress and expand the territories by acquiring new estates, landscaping vineyards, and encouraging the cultivation of orchards.

The castle was enlarged as well, and increasingly resembled a nobiliary abode: the rooms on the piano nobile were added to and remodeled, and the exterior of the building was refurbished.

Some of the records, drafted from the mid-seventeenth century, offer a more complete description of the palace, listing the number of apartments it was divided into: "The noble apartment, the women's apartment, the apartment in the middle and the visitors' apartment." There were living areas for the servants and facility rooms as well.

Upon the tragic death of her husband, who was murdered in 1608, Ottavia, alone and with two of her five children who were still young, took over the management of the family estate. Ottavia was a cultivated, sensitive woman who knew little about intrigue and weapons, and deserves credit for the creation of the garden in 1611, as we are reminded by the inscription that is still visible today on the portal at the entrance. There are those who believe, however, that the garden had already been planted before that date, probably in the late sixteenth century. Vignanello represents one of the most evocative examples of a Renaissance garden and one that has remained practically unchanged over time, also due to the fact that it has always belonged to the same family. Although it was created in the early seventeenth century, the garden does not seem to have been influenced by the parterres of French provenance, which had already begun to embroider the fronts of villas with their typical arabesques, and were destined to spread throughout Italy as well, but not until the end of the century.

Situated at the top of a hill on the other side of the moat, and behind the palazzo, the soil in the garden was leveled and an embankment was produced with backfill; a bridge built over the moat connected the garden to the palace. The leveled soil was then neatly arranged into twelve sections, consisting of hedges with a mixture of bay laurel tree, viburnum, boxwood, and cherry laurel. Inside these outer hedges, shorter boxwood hedges drew geometric patterns, which in the flower-beds in the middle included the heraldic rose of the Orsini family, Ottavia Orsini's initials, as well as those of her children, Sforza and Galeazzo. A fountain made of peperino, a typical material found locally, marked the heart of the garden.

Just beyond, and in continuity with the garden, is the so-called Marescotta estate, where fruit trees were cultivated inside flower-beds bordered by evergreen shrubs. The types of plants that were cultivated there are described in the writings of Clarice Marescotti, born in Vignanello in March 1598, and forced by her father to join an enclosed religious order. Initially, the little girl rebelled, but her attitude eventually changed and she ended up devoting her life to helping others, and after her death she was proclaimed a saint. Clarice was in charge of the convent vegetable garden, and in her letters to her brother, Vicino Sforza, she would reminisce about all the species that had grown at home: pomegranates, quinces, apples, pears, plums, and medlars.

On the southern side of the complex, on a terrace placed at a lower level, there was a secret garden, which the records describe as having flowers, citrus plants in vases, fountains and water features. Also located in the secret garden were storage areas and an oil press. Vases of citrus plants adorned the upper garden as well, and during the winter season they were sheltered by makeshift structures consisting of "lattice looms."

The estate extended southwards beyond the palazzo, where the

The garden is at the level of the piano nobile in the castle, connected to it by a bridge

View of a path in the garden

On the following spread
View of the garden. In the flower-beds in the middle, to the right is the rose of the Orsini and in the center the initials of Ottavia Orsini. In the foreground at the center are the initials of Ottavia's children, Sforza Vicino and Galeazzo. Just beyond the formal garden is the path of hedges crossing the orchard

so-called *barchetto* with fish pond and fountains was located. From there, one could cross the threshold to reach the *barco* with the animals used for the hunt. In turn, this area stretched even further south and, following the shape of the land, it occupied a vast portion of territory. It was crossed by a central path and had access doors. The inventories drafted in late 1600 also recorded the presence of an area where one could play tennis (*pallacorda*) as well as an aviary.

Sforza Vicino, Ottavia's son, married Vittoria Ruspoli in 1616. The bride's brother Bartolomeo designated their son Alessandro be his universal heir, on the condition that he take the house and the coat of arms of the Ruspoli. In the following years, the new Ruspoli Marescotti house was devoted to important projects that did not just concern their direct properties, but also involved redesigning the hamlet. The works, in addition to the maintenance of the palazzo and the gardens, involved repairing the roads, and planting elms and oaks all along them. They also involved erecting new buildings and factories: this activity gave rise to an important new urban design that was completed at the start of the following century, when the old houses, by that time dilapidated, were replaced by new ones, neatly arranged along the various streets, radically renewing the hamlet's appearance.

The revival of classical language and the renewed interest in geometric design and the Italian Renaissance garden began to catch on in America in the late nineteenth century, and then spread to Europe in the early twentieth, especially to England, and from there to the Tuscan hills, where a large group of foreigners, especially English and American ones, had settled.

Reinterpreting the Renaissance

Villa I Tatti

Artists, literati, wealthy members

of the middle class and eccentric figures devoted themselves to the restoration of ancient historic gardens and their related dwellings, or to the planning of others *ex novo*, drawing inspiration from Renaissance models. Within this environment of study and the rediscovery of Italian forms was the architect Cecil Pinsent, the artificer of numerous projects, especially in Tuscany. After arriving in Italy in 1907, Pinsent settled in Florence, a guest of the Houghton family, where he became close friends with the architecture historian Geoffrey Scott, who was also the librarian of Bernard Berenson, the renowned American historian. Berenson's wife, Mary, commissioned the two men to remodel the villa and the garden of the Tatti. From the start, the two intellectuals worked in harmony, thanks also to their complementary personalities: Geoffrey's brilliant literary culture was matched by the practical creativity of Cecil, who was well-versed in the technical aspects of their work. The intellectual contents conceived by Scott, who during his stay at I Tatti was writing his book *Architettura dell'Umanesimo*, came alive thanks to Pinsent's architectural culture. Both men moved to the villa to oversee the making of the library and the kitchens, and starting in 1910 they began doing the same for the work on the garden. I Tatti is organized according to a structure featuring closed spaces: just outside the villa is a small formal garden located between the residential building and the lemonary located across from it. Located past the lemonary are four geometric terraces, made out of boxwood and crossed by a central path, that slope toward the valley and end in a meadow. All is order and symmetry in the garden: the geometric compartments are not conceived merely to evoke the original model of the Renaissance garden, but so that their great potential can be perceived. The vision of the order that is hidden in nature becomes manifest thanks to the architecture,

and from the initial perception of the whole it can be
broken up into the individual geometric elements
that it is composed of, and that once again assume
a global view. The careful and calculated study of the
visuals was supposed to allow for a vision of the whole
and of the parts at the same time, assembling and
taking apart the total while perceiving the details,
but without ever losing sight of the whole. The layout
of the garden also suggests an exhaustive knowledge
of Renaissance models on the part of Pinsent, who in
the Belvedere, especially at the Villa d'Este in Tivoli,
found two important points of reference. Akin to Tivoli,
the English architect took advantage of the unevenness
of the ground in order to render the scenic effect of the
terraces and of the stairways that make the straight
path of the central axis less steep and more varied.

I Tatti, the staircase
climbing down toward
a wood filled with holm
oaks. In the background,
the villa and the formal
garden

I Tatti, the polychrome
stone floors are
a nod to the art
of the Renaissance

I Tatti, view of the formal
garden

Although Pinsent admitted his knowledge of and reference to the Renaissance model, he still managed to be independent, developing a personal language that moved him away from a mere reproduction and that led him to create new and original spaces instead. His collaboration with Scott continued until 1917, when Pinsent went his own way after completing Villa Le Balze, which he had designed with his friend. The young art historian had indeed married Lady Sybil Cutting, an English noblewoman and a friend of the Berenson, who had settled in Tuscany in 1910 after the death of her first husband, William Bayard Cutting. However, although Pinsent and Scott no longer worked together, they remained close friends. Pinsent continued to devote himself to his profession, and between 1927 and 1939 he made what is generally considered to be his masterpiece: Villa La Foce, lying on the slope of the hill, commissioned from him by the Marchese Origo. Although the garden was designed in four different stages, the overall plan was not affected and it in any case appears to be coherent and cohesive. The first formal garden just opposite the villa, made in 1927, consists of a fountain encircled by geometric boxwood hedges and bordered to the south by a wall. Just beyond this first garden is another, the Giardino di Limoni (Lemon Garden), which was begun in 1933, divided into boxwood compartments embellished at the corners by hemispheres and dotted with neatly arranged vases of citrus plants in the warmer seasons. Uphill from the Giardino di Limoni is a bower with wisteria: from there a row of cypresses begins, leading to the hilltop. Beyond the bower, over a long and narrow area is a rose garden. The final work at the Villa La Foce was carried out in 1939 and extended beyond the Giardino di Limoni, where Pinsent created a splendid geometric garden in a triangular shape defined by pruned cypresses, and including three rows of geometric compartments arranged in a fan shape. It can be accessed through

the Giardino di Limoni by way of a stairway made
of travertine extracted from the Rapolano quarries,
in the province of Siena. Below the main hall is a
grotto featuring a fountain. The scenography ends
at the top of the triangle, with an octagonal tub beyond
which there is a bench with a sculptural composition
on top of it. The garden layout is entirely modulated,
based on the careful balance between fulls and voids,
light and shadow, which accentuate the geometric
shapes harmoniously set in the Tuscan landscape.
Pinsent continued to work and design his gardens
until the outbreak of the Second World War,
whereupon he returned to London. In spite of this,
he still kept up his contacts with Italy and traveled
there, until he retired in Switzerland, where he lived
until he died in 1963.

View of the La Foce
complex

The wisteria arbor
in the lemon orchard

The composition of the
Foce terraces ends with
a beautiful triangular
terrace surrounded
by tall cypress hedges

BIBLIOGRAPHY

A. Palladio, *I quattro libri dell'Architettura*,
presso Dominico de' Franceschi, Venice 1570.
F. Pona, *Sileno*, Angelo Tamo in Verona, 1620.
A. Vallotto, *Giardino Giusti*, Collana Le Guide,
Edizioni di Vita Veronese, Verona 1955.
G. Masson, *Giardini d'Italia*, Milan 1961.
C. Perogalli, G.C. Bescapè, *Ville milanesi*, Milan 1965.
A. Ballarin, "La decorazione ad affresco della villa veneta
nel quinto decennio del Cinquecento: la villa
di Luvigliano," *Bollettino CISA*, no. X, 1968, pp. 115–26.
G. Marchini, *La villa imperiale di Pesaro*, Amilcare Pizzi,
Milan 1968.
K. Oberhuber, "Gli affreschi di Paolo Veronese nella villa
Barbaro," *Bollettino CISA*, no. X, 1968, pp. 188–202.
S. Langé, *Ville della provincia di Milano. Lombardia 4*,
Edizioni SISAR, Milan 1972.
O. Rossi-Pinelli, "La villa Imperiale di Pesaro come spazio
scenico per la corte urbinate," *Bollettino CISA*, no. XVI,
1974, pp. 219–33.
W. Lotz, "Il tempietto di Maser: note e riflessioni,"
Bollettino CISA, no. XIX, 1977, pp. 125–34.
J.S. Ackerman, *Palladio*, Einaudi, Turin 1978.
D. Lewis, "Il significato della decorazione plastica e
pittorica a Maser," *Bollettino CISA*, no. XXII, 1980,
pp. 203–13.
M. Fagiolo (ed.), *Natura e Artificio*, Rome 1981.
T.A. Marder, "La dedica e la funzione del Tempietto
di Palladio a Maser," *Bollettino CISA*, no. XXIII, 1981,
pp. 241–46.
G. Torselli, *Castelli e ville del Lazio*, Palombi Editori,
Rome 1983.
C.L. Frommel (ed.), *Raffaello architetto*, Electa,
Milan 1984.
A.M. Conforti Calcagni, "Villa Della Torre di Fumane
e i suoi problemi attributivi," *Annuario storico della
Valpolicella*, vol. 3, 1984–85, pp. 55–56.
M. Azzi Visentini, "La grotta nel Cinquecento Veneto:
il giardino Giusti di Verona," *Arte Veneta*, XXXIX, 1985,
pp. 55–64.
A. Conforti Calcagni, "Il giardino del Cinquecento: dal
Sacro Bosco di Bomarzo al giardino Giusti di Verona,"
Civiltà Veronese, I, 1985, pp. 34–48.
A. Morandotti, "Nuove tracce per il tardo Rinascimento
italiano: il ninfeo-museo della villa Borromeo, Visconti
Borromeo, Litta, Toselli di Lainate," *Annali della Scuola
Normale Superiore di Pisa*, Series III, vol. 15, no. 1, 1985,
pp. 129–85.

M. Azzi Visentini (ed.), *Il giardino veneto: storia
e conservazione*, Mondadori Electa, Milan 1988.
P. Brugnoli, A. Sandrini (eds.), *L'architettura a Verona
nell'età della Serenissima (sec. XV-XVIII)*, Banca Popolare
di Verona-Mondadori, Verona 1988.
H. Bredekamp, W. Janzer, *Vicino Orsini e il Bosco Sacro
di Bomarzo. Un principe artista e anarchico*, Edizioni
dell'Elefante, Rome 1989.
D. Battilotti, *Le ville di Palladio*, Mondadori Electa,
Milan 1990.
M. Mosser, G. Teyssot (eds.), *L'architettura dei giardini
d'Occidente: dal Rinascimento al Novecento*,
Mondadori Electa, Milan 1990.
S. Eiche, *Prologue to the Villa Imperiale Frescoes*,
Urbino 1991.
A. Tagliolini, *Storia del giardino Italiano*, Ponte alle Grazie,
Florence 1991.
J.S. Ackerman, *La villa: forma e ideologia*, Einaudi,
Turin 1992.
L. Franzoni, "Le Muse, il piacere, la virtù e l'onore a
confronto nel giardino Giusti," *Atti e Memorie della
Accademia di Agricoltura Scienze e Lettere di Verona*,
Verona 1992.
F. Nuvolari (ed.), *Il giardino storico all'italiana*, conference
proceedings, Milan 1992.
A. Campitelli, *La Rocca ed il Borgo di Vignanello dai
Farnese ai Ruspoli*, in "La dimensione europea dei
Farnese", *Bulletin de l'Institut historique Belgique
de Rome*, LXII/1993.
A. Sandrini, *Villa Della Torre a Fumane*, Banca Agricola
Popolare di Cerea, Verona 1993.
S. Varoli Piazza, *Giardino, Barchetto e Barco della Rocca
Ruspoli a Vignanello*, in "La dimensione europea
dei Farnese", *Bulletin de l'Institut historique Belgique
de Rome*, LXII/1993.
P. Cottini, *Giardini di Lombardia, dalle origini all'età
barocca*, Edizioni Lativa, Varese 1994.
O. Guaita, *Le ville della Lombardia*, Mondadori Electa,
Milan 1994.
G. Conforti, "Le grotte veronesi nei giardini di villa: miti
inganni e labirinti," *Annuario storico della Valpolicella*,
1994–95, pp. 31–66.
*Il ninfeo di villa Visconti Borromeo Litta a Lainate. Progetto
di valorizzazione e restauro*, Lainate 1996.
M. Azzi Visentini, *La villa in Italia: Quattrocento
e Cinquecento*, Mondadori Electa, Milan 1997.
G. Conforti, F. Legnaghi, "Dalla Domus seu palacium

all'attuale conformazione di Villa della Torre a Fumane," *Annuario storico della Valpolicella*, 1997–98, pp. 116–54.

C.L. Frommel, T.F. Fagliari Zeni Buchicchio, "Il Palazzo Orsini a Bomarzo: opera di Baldassarre Peruzzi," *Römisches Jahrbuch der Bibliotheca Hertziana"*, vol. 32, 1997–98, pp. 7–134.

M. Fantoni, H. Flores, J. Pfordresher (eds.), *Cecil Pinsent and his gardens in Tuscany*, Edifir, Florence 1999.

C. Acidini Luchinat (ed.), *Giardini Medicei: giardini di palazzo e di villa nella Firenze del Quattrocento*, Motta, Milan 2000.

G. Beltramini, A. Padoan (eds.), *Andrea Palladio: Atlante delle architetture*, Marsilio, Venice 2000.

M. Calvesi, *Gli incantesimi di Bomarzo: il sacro bosco tra arte e letteratura*, Bompiani, Milan 2000.

P. Lanaro, P. Marini, G.M. Varanini (eds.), *Edilizia privata nella Verona rinascimentale: convegno di studi*, Verona, September 24–26, 1998, with the assistance of Edoardo Demo, Milan 2000.

S. Varoli Piazza, *Paesaggi e giardini della Tuscia*, De Luca, Rome 2000.

V. Cazzato, M. Fagiolo, M.A. Giusti (eds.), *Atlante delle grotte e dei ninfei in Italia: Toscana, Lazio, Italia meridionale e isole*, Mondadori Electa, Milan 2001.

E. Benzo, A. Anzani, C. Pagani, *Villa Borromeo Visconti Litta a Lainate. Arte, storia, cultura, architettura e giardini, restauro*, Lainate 2002.

V. Cazzato, M. Fagiolo, M.A. Giusti (eds.), *Atlante delle grotte e dei ninfei in Italia: Italia settentrionale, Umbria e Marche*, Mondadori Electa, Milan 2002.

G. Conforti, "Villa Della Torre: l'architettura, i mostri, il tempietto. Iconografia di un itinerario morale nel Cinquecento," *Annuario storico della Valpolicella*, 2002–03, pp. 241–66.

A. Bruschi (ed.), *Storia dell'Architettura Italiana, il primo Cinquecento*, Mondadori Electa, Milan 2003.

C. Iuozzo, *Feudatari e vassalli a Vignanello*, Agnesotti, Viterbo 2003.

L. Donadono (ed.), *Bomarzo: architetture fra natura e società*, Gangemi, Rome 2004.

A. Pinelli, *La bellezza impura: arte e politica nell'Italia del Rinascimento*, Laterza, Rome 2004.

G. Beltramini, H. Burns (eds.), *Andrea Palladio e la villa veneta da Petrarca a Carlo Scarpa*, exhibition catalogue (Vicenza, March 5 – July 3, 2005), Marsilio, Venice 2005.

S. Frommel (ed.), *Villa Lante a Bagnaia*, Mondadori Electa, Milan 2005.

A. Morandotti, *Milano profana nell'età dei Borromeo*, Mondadori Electa, Milan 2005.

A. Conforti Calcagni, *Bellissima è dunque la rosa, i giardini dalle signorie alla Serenissima*, Il Saggiatore, Milan 2006.

F.R. Liserre, *Giardini anglo-fiorentini: il Rinascimento all'inglese di Cecil Pinsent*, Pontecorboli Editore, Florence 2008.

L. Miotto, *Villa imperiale di Pesaro: Girolamo Genga*, Marsilio, Venice 2008.

C.E. Spantigati (ed.), *Delle cacce ti dono il sommo impero: restauri per la Sala di Diana alla Venaria Reale*, Nardini, Turin 2008.

F. Ceccarelli, M. Folin (eds.), *Delizie estensi: architetture di villa nel Rinascimento italiano ed europeo*, Olschki, Florence 2009.

S. Frommel (ed.), *Bomarzo: il sacro bosco*, Mondadori Electa, Milan 2009.

G. Simoncini (ed.), *Roma: le trasformazioni urbane nel Cinquecento. Dalla città al territorio*, vol. 2, Olschki, Florence 2011.

L. Borromeo Dina (ed.), *Villa dei Vescovi*, Edibus Comunicazione, Vicenza 2012.

H. Burns, *La villa italiana del Rinascimento*, Colla Editore, Novara 2012.

G. Beltramini, D. Gasparotto, A. Tura (eds.), *Pietro Bembo e l'invenzione del Rinascimento: Mantegna, Bellini, Giorgione, Tiziano, Raffaello*, exhibition catalogue (Padua, February 2 – May 19, 2013), Venice 2013.

P. Brugnoli, *Villa Della Torre a Fumane di Valpolicella*, Antiga Edizioni, Verona 2013.

S. Varoli Piazza, *Ville e giardini storici della Tuscia/ Villas and Historic Gardens of Tuscia*, Ginevra Bentivoglio, Rome 2015.

A. Conforti Calcagni, *Il giardino Giusti*, Cierre Edizioni, Verona 2016.

S. Desmond, *Gardens of the italian lakes*, Frances Lincoln Ltd., London 2016.

G. Agosti, J. Stoppa (eds.), *Un seminario sul manierismo in Lombardia*, Officina Libraria, Milan 2017.

M. Cogni, *Villa Cicogna Mozzoni*, Officina Libraria, Milan 2019.

Cover: View of Villa Cicogna Mozzoni
with its Renaissance garden

Translation: Sylvia Adrian Notini

Graphic Design: Cristina Menotti

© 2019 Mondadori Electa S.p.A., Milan
All rights reserved
First edition: November 2019

www.electa.it

Distributed in English throughout the World
by Rizzoli International Publications Inc.
300 Park Avenue South
New York, NY 10010, USA

ISO 9001
Mondadori Electa S.p.A. is certified for the Quality
Management System by Bureau Veritas Italia S.p.A.,
in compliance with UNI EN ISO 9001.

This book respects the environment
The paper used was produced using wood from forests
managed to strict environmental standards; the companies
involved guarantee sustainable production certified
environmentally.

This volume was printed at Lito Terrazzi Srl, Iolo
Printed in Italy